Qurick & Healthy

Recipes for
Vibrant Living

by Julian Whitaker, M.D.
and the Whitaker Wellness Institute
Nutrition Team

Quick&Healthy

Qurick&Healthy

Table of Contents

Optimal Health

a reality, not a dream

Optimal Health
a reality, not a dream

Good nutrition is key to optimal health. Unfortunately, many people are confused about the best approach to diet. Have you been put off by all the conflicting claims and controversies of various diets? Do you shy away from programs that require a mathematics degree to figure out calories and portion sizes? Have you tried eating "health food" and found it tasteless and boring?

Rest assured that well-balanced eating need not be complicated or drab. In this cookbook, we offer you easy-to-prepare recipes for mouth-watering dishes, developed by the Whitaker Wellness Institute's team of nutrition experts. Unlike extreme regimens that call for severe restriction of a certain food group such as fats or carbohydrates, our recommended recipes are pretty "normal." There are no specific items you have to eat in abundance, nor is anything completely off limits. As a result, because you have access to your own personal favorites among a variety of fresh, tasty, nutritious foods, you'll find it easy to make this cookbook your mainstay.

Optimal health is a goal that all of us share. The new Quick & Healthy cookbook that you are about to start using is a tool that can help you achieve this goal.

To your health,

About Julian Whitaker, MD

Julian Whitaker, MD, graduated from Dartmouth College and Emory University Medical School. During his orthopedic surgery residency at the University of California San Francisco, Dr. Whitaker became interested in something he was never taught in medical school: nutrition and its impact on health. He soon became convinced that a more natural approach to medicine held far more promise than conventional medicine's blunt tools of prescription drugs and surgery.

As he delved into the research on diet, exercise and nutritional supplements – and witnessed firsthand the healing powers of these simple therapies – his medical career took an abrupt turn. In 1979, Dr. Whitaker opened the Whitaker Wellness Institute Medical Clinic. Over the years, more than 30,000 patients have gone through the clinic's Back to Health Program, a comprehensive approach to treating illness and restoring health. At the clinic, patients undergo thorough medical evaluation and are treated with safe, proven therapies that are ignored by conventional medicine. They also participate in an intensive educational program to learn the nuts and bolts of lifestyle change, with special emphasis on nutrition and diet.

Dr. Whitaker has also been a driving force in alternative medicine for the past 25 years. He has written eight books, given hundreds of lectures and interviews on national radio and TV, and is the author of the popular monthly newsletter, *Health & Healing*.

For more information on Dr. Whitaker's clinic, please contact:

Whitaker Wellness Institute
4321 Birch Street
Newport Beach, CA 92660
800/488-1500
whitakerwellness.com

For information on *Health & Healing*, contact:
Phillips Health
800/539-8219
drwhitaker.com

Acknowledgements

Like most projects, putting together *Quick & Healthy Recipes for Vibrant Living* has been a group effort, and I would like to acknowledge the key players on the Whitaker Wellness Institute Nutrition Team.

The bulk of the recipes were provided by Peggy Dace, Research Director of the Whitaker Wellness Institute, and Teresa Herring, Senior Managing Editor of my newsletter *Health & Healing*. These two spent countless hours putting their heads together to come up with these recipes, testing and modifying them – not an easy task when you consider that one of them lives in California and the other in Maryland. Recipes were also supplied by Idel Kelly, who has been the chef at the Whitaker Wellness Institute for the past 20 years, clinical nutritionist Diane Lara, and Connie Whitaker, my wife and inspiration.

A special thanks to Randolph Mann, who edited each and every recipe and ended up testing more than a few of them. He also supplied the all-important nutritional analysis of each recipe. Randy's attention to detail, passion for food, and vast experience – he has written and edited several cookbooks, run a cooking school and worked as a chef – brought a much-appreciated level of expertise to this endeavor.

I would also like to acknowledge the following people: Howard Cohl and Peter Dombrowski of Silverback Books, who approached us with the idea of writing this cookbook; Tom Callahan and Glynnis Mileikowsky of Phillips Health, who helped put the details together; Tracey and Andy Thornley of Scoot Design for their beautiful design work; and Suzanne Carreiro and Lisa Keegan for their amazing food styling and photography.

Everyone involved would like to thank their families and friends who served as guinea pigs and tasters. We all hope you like this cookbook as much as we do.

Julian Whitaker MD

Julian Whitaker, MD, and the
Whitaker Wellness Institute Nutrition Team

Principles of the *Quick & Healthy Cookbook* Recipes

An underlying objective of the *Quick & Healthy Cookbook* is to free you up from the little things – and the big things – that put a damper on your life. First, let's get free of the food preparation rut so many of us fall into over the years. Use this cookbook to broaden your horizons and inspire you to try different, healthful foods and methods of cooking.

Free yourself from the worries of menu planning. Let the recipes in this book do the work for you. Select a hearty soup, salad or entrée that suits your palate and build a meal around it. Many of the main dishes are a perfect blend of vegetable, starch, and protein, so extra dishes are often not necessary. Map out a few days' worth of menus in advance so you can gather needed ingredients in one shopping trip.

The balanced recipes in this book will, little by little, free you of unwanted pounds. You'll eat heartily, but because you'll be cutting back on high-calorie fats and refined carbohydrates, your overall caloric intake will fall. Furthermore, because the foods we recommend have a regulating effect on blood sugar, you'll feel full longer – no more episodes of extreme hunger when you eat yourself out of house and home. The result will be effortless weight loss.

Above all, the goal of this cookbook is to help you adopt a style of eating that frees you of disease. Food is powerful medicine. Do not underestimate the healing qualities and rejuvenating power of nutrition. Encourage yourself by making note of even small improvements in your well-being: more restful sleep, less heartburn, no pounding heart after climbing a flight of stairs, a looser waistband, fewer mood swings, more energy... Expect change. Look forward to it.

Free yourself from the ailments that restrict you. You'll be thankful that you invested the effort.

This is a chance for you to begin experiencing the benefits of the Whitaker Wellness Institute program in your own home. Discover why tens of thousands who have gone through the Back to Health Program at the institute have made remarkable strides in restoring and maintaining health. Here is an overview of the guiding principles underlying the recipes in this book.

Eat the Right Kind of Carbs

Carbohydrates are your body's primary energy source. All carbohydrates are broken down in the digestive tract into glucose or other simple sugars, which are then absorbed into the bloodstream. This stimulates the pancreas to produce insulin, which ushers glucose into the cells. Glucose is used for energy, and excesses are converted into glycogen and stored in the liver and muscles for future use. When these storehouses are full, it is converted into fat and stored in fat cells.

Yet all carbohydrate foods are not broken down and absorbed at the same rate. Some, such as white potatoes and bread, are quickly converted to glucose and cause a rapid rise in blood sugar and insulin. Others, like beans, vegetables, and whole grains, are broken down more slowly and result in a lower and more gradual release of glucose.

The glycemic index is a ranking system of the rate at which various foods raise blood sugar. Foods like potatoes that cause a quick and high rise are classified as having a high glycemic index, while beans and other slow-burning foods have a low glycemic index. Fiber-rich, low-glycemic carbohydrate foods such as vegetables, fruits, beans, legumes, and whole grains should make up the bulk of your total calories, while high-glycemic flour, sugar, and other processed carbs should be eaten sparingly. (For a glycemic index of common foods, see the list on page 184.)

Protein in Moderation

Proteins are broken down by the digestive system into amino acids and released into the bloodstream. The body uses amino acids to synthesize proteins for cellular repair and growth, and as "functional proteins" like enzymes and hemoglobin. Unlike carbohydrates and fats, the body does not store proteins. Some are converted into metabolic fuels and used as energy, but most excess proteins are broken down into uric acid and urea and excreted in the urine.

While it is important to get adequate protein, don't go overboard. Eating too much protein is hard on the kidneys, and it can also contribute to osteoporosis and an increased risk of fracture. Furthermore, protein is most concentrated in meat, eggs and dairy products, which also contain saturated fat. The best protein sources include skinless poultry, fish, egg whites, low-fat or fat-free dairy products, tofu, beans and legumes, and whole grains. A 3-to 4-ounce serving of protein-rich food with every meal is plenty.

Good Fats, Bad Fats

During digestion, dietary fats are emulsified by bile acids into tiny units of fat. These fat particles are absorbed by the lymphatic system, released into the bloodstream, and carried to fat storage depots throughout the body. Fat is an integral nutrient. It cushions your organs, provides insulation, and is used for energy. It is also an important component of cellular membranes, as well as a precursor to chemical messengers called prostaglandins that have far-reaching effects in your body. There are three classes of fats, and they have different effects in the body.

SATURATED FATS, found mostly in meat, egg yolks, and dairy products, raise levels of harmful LDL cholesterol and encourage the platelets in the blood to stick together, thereby contributing to risk of heart disease. Eating some saturated fat is fine. For example, despite its reputation for being high in cholesterol, an egg a day is perfectly acceptable for most people. Eating lots of saturated fat is not.

MONOUNSATURATED FATS, found in olive oil as well as canola, hazelnut, and almond oils, are actually beneficial for the cardiovascular system. Olive oil is particularly healthful, and it is our cooking oil of choice. It has a long history of use and has been shown to protect against heart disease by keeping the arteries flexible and guarding against free radical damage. One of olive oil's best properties is that it is relatively stable and can tolerate moderate heat. When you're looking for a milder-flavored oil for baking, try hazelnut oil, which you'll find in your health food store.

POLYUNSATURATED FATS are among the most healthful of all oils, for they include the essential fatty acids, which cannot be produced in the body but must be obtained through diet. Polyunsaturated oils, such as walnut, corn, sunflower, and other vegetable oils, are quite fragile, so they do not make good cooking oils. Heating unleashes oxidative damage to their chemical structure and produces free radicals and other harmful byproducts. Purchase only unrefined, expeller-pressed oils from your health food store, store them in your refrigerator, and never heat them. Save them for salad dressings or add to dishes after cooking.

ESSENTIAL FATTY ACIDS (EFAs) are polyunsaturated fats that are involved in the formation of cellular membranes, brain function, inflammation, and chemical signaling. Omega-6 EFAs are found in nuts, seeds, and vegetable oils, so if you include these foods in your diet, you likely get adequate amounts of these crucial fats. Omega-3's (which include DHA, one of the most active fats in the brain, and EPA, which helps promote cardiovascular health) are abundant only in cold-water fish and flaxseed, so deficiencies are quite common. Try to eat omega-3-rich salmon, mackerel, sardines, and other cold-water fish two or three times a week, and use a quarter-cup of freshly ground flaxseed daily, sprinkled on your cereal or mixed in water or another drink.

TRANS FATS are the most damaging fats of all. Created as a byproduct of hydrogenation, a process that stabilizes polyunsaturated oils, trans fats raise LDL cholesterol, lower protective HDL cholesterol, and are linked to increased risk of heart disease, cancer, diabetes, infertility, and obesity. Read labels carefully and avoid anything made with partially hydrogenated oils (margarine, commercially baked goods, etc.), as well as foods that have been fried in vegetable oils (French fries and other deep-fried foods).

Nutrition Guidelines in a Nutshell

The general dietary guidelines of the Whitaker Wellness Institute nutrition program are straightforward and easy to implement. To take the guesswork out of knowing exactly what's going into your body, we have provided a thorough nutritional analysis with each and every recipe.

1. Make Low-Glycemic Carbohydrates the Foundation of Your Diet

The foundation of your diet, 50-60 percent of your total caloric intake, should be slow-burning vegetables, fruits, beans, and whole grains. These low-glycemic carbs are excellent sources of fiber, vitamins, minerals, antioxidants and protective phytonutrients. Eat these foods in as close to their natural state as possible. If you can find organic produce, go for it. At the same time, limit your intake of high-glycemic processed and refined grains.

2. Eat the Right Kinds of Fat

About 20-25 percent of your daily calories should come from healthy fats: olive oil, raw nuts, avocados, and fatty fish like salmon. Go easy on saturated fats and steer clear of processed trans fats. Use olive oil for cooking and enjoy cold-pressed polyunsaturated vegetable oils, but don't heat them. Use olive oil cooking spray to coat non-stick skillets, baking pans, and griddles. (Or get an oil mister and fill it with good oil.) A little organic butter now and then is perfectly acceptable.

3. Get Adequate, Low-Fat Protein

Eat a little fish, lean poultry, egg whites, low-fat dairy, soy or other beans with each meal, and you'll get plenty of protein. If you're eating red meat, make sure it's very lean to avoid getting much saturated fat in your diet. Ground turkey breast, Egg Beaters® or other egg white products, and skinless poultry (look for organically fed free-range poultry and cage-free eggs) are good protein substitutes for the usual fatty fare. Your daily protein intake should be about 20-25 percent of total calories.

4. Watch Your Portion Sizes

Average serving sizes have ballooned over the past two decades, a trend that has accompanied the ballooning of the waistline of the average American. We don't want you to have to constantly count calories or grams of fat - we've done that for you. You will, however, need to monitor your portions, and the guidelines below should help. If you're still hungry, eat more vegetables, beans, and whole grains. Eating slowly will also help you eat less.

Recommended Daily Intake and Portion Sizes

Carbohydrates (50-60 percent of total calories)

- Vegetables: 5-8 servings; limit starchy vegetables (white potatoes, turnips) to two to three times a week. 1 serving = 1 cup raw (the size of a tennis ball) or 3/4 cup cooked vegetables. If you need to eat more, eat from this food group.
- Fruit: 3-4 servings; go easy on dried fruits (dried apricots are okay). 1 serving = 1 medium whole fruit or 3/4 cup sliced fruit.
- Starches and grains: 3-4 servings of bread, cereal, pasta, or grain. 1 serving = 1 slice of bread, 1/2 bagel or 3/4 cup cooked cereal, pasta or grain. Beware: This is the easiest category of carbohydrates to overeat.

Protein (20-25 percent of total calories)

- 3-4 servings of lean protein
- Fish or poultry: 1 serving = 4 ounces (about the size of a deck of cards)
- Beans: 1 serving = 3/4 cup cooked beans
- Soy products: 1 serving = 4 ounces tofu, 1 cup soy milk, 1/2 cup soy protein
- Raw nuts and seeds: 1 serving = 2 tablespoons nuts, seeds or nut butter
- Dairy: 1 serving = 1 cup low-fat or nonfat cottage cheese or yogurt
- Eggs: 1 serving = 1 whole egg, 2 egg whites, or 1/4 cup Egg Beaters® or another frozen egg white product

Fat (20-25 percent of total calories)

- Trim meat, skin poultry, go easy on whole-fat dairy, and use primarily olive or other monounsaturated oils. Avoid fried foods and those made with partially hydrogenated oils (including margarine, regular peanut butter, and store-bought pastries and baked goods, and deep-fried foods).

23

Healthy Shopping List

Here are some of the items you will be using frequently. You don't have to buy everything listed here, but it is a good idea to keep a stock of staples on hand. You'll find most of these foods in your grocery store, but a few things will have to be purchased in a health food store.

Beans and Legumes

- Beans: garbanzo, white, red, navy, pink, black, black-eyed peas, pinto
- Long-grain brown rice
- Lentils
- Soybeans, raw in pod (called "edamame") (look in frozen foods)
- Split peas
- *Dried, frozen, and canned beans are all acceptable. (Rinse canned beans in a colander to remove excess sodium.)*

Breads

- Pita bread (sprouted-grain preferred)
- Pumpernickel and rye bread
- Rye Crisps and stone-ground whole-wheat crackers
- Sprouted-grain bread
- Tortillas, whole-wheat
- Whole-wheat bread (stone-ground best)
  Breads made with sprouted grains have the lowest glycemic rating. Next best are breads made from stone-ground whole grains. May be stored in freezer.

Cereals and Grains

- Bran flakes
- Bulgur (cracked wheat)
- Multi-grain hot cereal
- Oatmeal (not instant)
- Whole grains (wheat berries, oat groats, quinoa, barley, etc.)
- Whole wheat flour (stone-ground preferred)
  Cold cereals have a very high glycemic index. Hot cereals made from whole or flaked grains are much better.

Dairy/Eggs/Poultry/Fish/Meat Substitutes

- Cheese (use in moderation; keep grated Parmesan on hand)
- Chicken breasts, skinless (bags of boneless, skinless frozen breasts are handy)
- Cottage cheese, nonfat
- Eggs, preferably cage-free
- Egg Beaters® or other egg white products (avoid egg substitutes)
- Fish, your choice (fatty fish such as salmon, sardines, anchovies, mackerel, and trout are richest in omega-3 fatty acids)
- Ground turkey or chicken breast (lower in fat than regular ground chicken or turkey, which contains skin.)
- Milk, nonfat
- Soy meat substitutes (soy burgers, bacon, lunchmeats, and ground beef, found in the frozen or deli sections)
- Soymilk, low-fat
- Tofu (firm or extra-firm is easiest to work with)
- Turkey
- Yogurt, plain, nonfat

Condiments/Cooking Ingredients

- Arrowroot (a thickening agent, like cornstarch) or cornstarch
- Baking powder (aluminum-free)
- Baking soda
- Brown rice syrup (low-glycemic, syrupy sweetener)
- Cardia Salt (has half the sodium as salt, along with potassium, magnesium, and lysine)
- Cornstarch
- Flaxseed oil (store in refrigerator)
- Herbs and spices (fresh is best; dried acceptable)
- Ketchup (low-sugar)
- Mustard
- NuSalt (potassium chloride salt substitute: 1/8 teaspoon contains 500 milligrams potassium and no sodium)
- Olive oil, extra-virgin
- Stevia (herbal sweetener available in powder or liquid)
- Tapioca
- Vanilla extract
- Vinegar (balsamic, apple cider, and/or wine)
- Xylitol (a low-glycemic sweetener derived from birch trees; may be used in baking)

Fruits

- Applesauce, unsweetened
- Apricots, dried (other dried fruits have a very high glycemic index)
- Fresh fruits
- Frozen fruits packed without sugar (berries, cherries, peaches, etc.)

Nuts and Seeds

- Raw nuts and seeds, all types
- Raw nut butters (almond is particularly nice)

Pastas

- All pastas (with the exception of gnocchi and pastas stuffed with high-fat cheese)

Vegetables

- Fresh vegetables (use starchy root vegetables such as potatoes, turnips, and parsnips in moderation)
- Frozen vegetables (without sauces or excess salt)
- Canned vegetables (rinse well to remove sodium)

getting started

You won't need a lot of specialized equipment to make the recipes in this cookbook, but one thing you will need is non-stick cookware. You'll be using far less oil than you might be used to, and non-stick cookwear makes this much easier. Several recipes call for a blender or food processor, and a few suggest using a microwave, although this is certainly not a necessity.

If you cook regularly, you will have no problem with the recipes and cooking methods detailed in this cookbook. You will quickly adapt to and even improve upon the suggested recipes to custom fit your tastes. If you are an inexperienced cook, any kind of cooking is going to be a challenge at first. The good news is that our recipes tend to be easier to prepare than those in many other cookbooks.

Our recipes might, however, challenge some of your eating habits. We know that making changes in your diet isn't easy, and at first glance, your confidence level may not be at its highest. This is a normal reaction to any kind of change. One thing that will make it easier is to always keep your eye on your goal of better health. After just a few weeks of making use of the recipes in this cookbook, you will begin to understand – and feel – how this nutrition program can improve your health and actually prevent and reverse many of the risk factors for disease facing us today. Your health goals are within your reach, and the time to start down the road to optimal health is now.

Good luck, bon vivant and bon appétit!

Start Your Day

The breakfasts that await you were designed with three things in mind.

- Quick and easy preparation. The last thing you need in the morning is complicated recipes. You can throw most of these breakfasts together in minutes, so you're guaranteed to stay cool and get to work on time.

- Healthy and hearty. After just a few days of starting your day on a sound nutritional footing, you'll notice increased energy, mental alertness, and satiety throughout the morning.

- Fresh and satisfying. Say goodbye to cold cereal and toast and look forward to delicious, tasty morning meals.

firing on all cylinders

As a meal, breakfast often gets no respect. On weekdays in particular, it's usually whatever is quick and convenient, with little thought to how what you eat affects how you feel and how you function.

What you choose for breakfast will determine whether you feel alert, focused, and satiated until lunch. Slow-burning carbohydrates and moderate amounts of protein are your best bets. Use the glycemic index (page 184) as your guide when choosing your food; for example, pick a piece of fruit over a glass of juice to prevent quick ups and downs in your blood sugar and energy levels. When it comes to bread, stick to sprouted-grain or stone-ground whole wheat products. And while hot cereals made from whole grains are excellent, many cold cereals can send your blood sugar on a roller coaster ride that can leave you fatigued and unfocused. If you're a fan of cold cereal, the best are those made from bran.

For an extra health boost, grind one-fourth cup of flaxseed and sprinkle it on cooked or cold cereal for extra fiber, protein and heart-healthy omega-3 fatty acids.

Orchard Pancakes

Soluble fiber, insoluble fiber, and great taste all in one.

Makes 2 servings, four to five pancakes
½ medium apple, peeling optional
2 egg whites
2 tablespoons soy flour
½ teaspoon cinnamon
½ teaspoon vanilla
2 slices sprouted-grain or
stone-ground whole wheat bread
½ cup nonfat milk or soy milk
½ teaspoon baking soda
Olive oil spray, as needed
For garnish: thin slices of pear or apple

Cut the apple into chunks and put it in a blender or food processor with egg whites, soy flour, cinnamon, and vanilla. Blend until apple is well pureed. With blender running, add small bits of bread alternately with milk. Last of all, add soda and continue to blend one full minute until mixture is smooth. Onto a hot griddle sprayed with olive oil, pour enough batter to spread into a six-inch circle that is about ¼ inch thick. Watch carefully as browning occurs quickly. Turn and brown other side. On the same griddle, lightly sauté thin fruit slices for garnish. Serve with brown rice syrup and Vanilla Cream (recipe on p. 48) or Blueberry Spread (recipe below).

TIME NEEDED: 25 minutes

Per Serving: Calories 189, Total Fat 6gr (Sat 1g, Mono 4g, Poly 1g) Cholesterol 1mg, Sodium 415mg, Carbs 21g, Fiber 4g, Protein 10g.

Blueberry Spread

No matter how you spread it, it's mighty fine eating.

Makes 2 cups
2 cups unsweetened frozen blueberries
2 to 6 drops stevia (to taste)
1 teaspoon vanilla
Pinch of nutmeg

Heat and simmer blueberries in saucepan. Remove from heat; stir in stevia, vanilla, and nutmeg. Serve warm, over waffles, pancakes, or cereal.

Variation: Replace some of the blueberries with another fruit such as chopped fresh apple or peach. Adjust sweetening to taste.

TIME NEEDED: 15 minutes

Per ½ cup: Calories 43, Total Fat tr (Sat tr, Mono tr, Poly tr) Cholesterol 0mg, Sodium 1mg, Carbs 10g, Fiber 2g, Protein tr.

THE DOCTOR IS IN:

Blueberries have the highest antioxidant levels of all fruits and vegetables. Their intense color comes from pigments called anthocyanins, which have been shown to improve circulation and night vision, and generally enhance the health of the eyes.

Stick-To-Your-Ribs Hot Cereal

Say hello to consistent energy through the entire morning.

Makes 3 servings

1 cup whole grain(s)*
2 to 3 cups water (as directed)
*Oatmeal, barley, wheat kernels, buckwheat groats, teff, multi-grain cereal, quinoa (a South American native that contains very high-quality protein), or other whole grains

In a heavy saucepan over medium heat, bring water (amount suggested per package instructions) to a boil. Add grains, reduce heat to a simmer, cover and cook as directed. Cooking times range from 15 minutes for quinoa and oatmeal to an hour for wheat kernels. Top with Banana Topping (recipe follows). Another nice topping is 1/2 cup chopped dried apricots, almond extract (1/8 to 1/4 teaspoon), and 1/4 cup chopped almonds.

TIME NEEDED: Varies according to the grain.

✳ Cook's Notes: A quick and easy way to prepare hot cereal is in a wide-mouthed thermos. Before you go to bed at night, place 2 cups boiling water and 1 cup whole grains in thermos. Amount of water may vary from grain to grain. Close thermos and let sit overnight. In the morning, you will have warm, cooked cereal. Even if you decide to cook it more on the stovetop, this will greatly reduce cooking time.

Per Serving: Calories 104, Total Fat 2gr (Sat tr, Mono 1g, Poly 1g) Cholesterol 0mg, Sodium 1mg, Carbs 18g, Fiber 3g, Protein 4g.

Banana Topping

A great way to get blood pressure-lowering potassium.

Makes 3 servings

1½ cups nonfat milk or soy milk
2 medium bananas, barely ripe
1½ teaspoons vanilla
¼ teaspoon cinnamon (optional)

Combine ingredients in a blender or food processor until smooth. Serve with Stick-to-Your-Ribs Hot Cereal. Also great on French toast, pancakes, or waffles.

TIME NEEDED: 5 minutes

Per Serving: Calories 149, Total Fat 1gr (Sat tr, Mono tr, Poly tr) Cholesterol 2mg, Sodium 64mg, Carbs 25g, Fiber 2g, Protein 5g.

Gourmet Pecan Pancakes

Try the head-start trick explained below. It makes breakfast easier and produces a superior pancake.

Makes about 12 pancakes

2 cups whole wheat flour*

3 teaspoons baking powder

½ teaspoon salt or salt substitute

1 tablespoon xylitol

1 egg

1¼ cups nonfat milk*

¾ cup chopped pecans

Preheat a nonstick griddle or large skillet over medium-high heat. Mix flour, baking powder, salt, and xylitol together in a large mixing bowl, stirring until well blended. Beat egg and milk in a small mixing bowl, then pour into dry ingredients. Stir until just moistened. Spray griddle or pan with olive oil spray, then pour batter onto grill, using about 1/4 cup for each pancake. As pancakes begin to set, sprinkle 1 tablespoon of pecans over each one. Turn and continue cooking until done. Serve with brown rice syrup.

*If you have time, start these before you go to bed. Mix only the flour and milk together, cover the bowl and put it in the refrigerator. Then in the morning, add the rest of the ingredients. A touch more milk can be added if you like thinner pancakes. Making an overnight sponge produces a beautiful texture.

TIME NEEDED: 10 minutes preparation, plus cooking time.

Per 2 hotcakes: Calories 264, Total Fat 10gr (Sat 1g, Mono 6g, Poly 3g) Cholesterol 32mg, Sodium 370mg, Carbs 37g, Fiber 6g, Protein 9g.

THE DOCTOR IS IN:

Nuts have a bad rap. True, they contain a lot of calories and fat, but this doesn't mean they're not good for you. In fact, eating nuts has been shown to lower the risk of heart disease. Nuts are a great source of heart-healthy monounsaturated and polyunsaturated fats. They are also rich in vitamin E, a potent antioxidant, and arginine, an amino acid that improves blood flow. Eat your nuts raw whenever possible, for roasting damages their fragile polyunsaturated fats.

Orange And Brandy French Toast

Like champagne brunch at the Ritz but pocketbook and health-friendly.

Makes 2 servings

1 whole egg

1 egg white

2 tablespoons soy milk or nonfat milk

Grated rind of one large orange

1 tablespoon brandy

(or one teaspoon vanilla extract)

½ teaspoon vanilla

½ teaspoon cinnamon

4 slices sprouted grain bread

Put all the ingredients, except the bread, in a small mixing bowl. Whisk until well blended and pour into shallow pan.

Coat bread evenly in the mixture. Brown both sides, using a fairly hot skillet or griddle lightly sprayed with olive oil spray.

Serve with brown rice syrup or Berry Syrup (recipe below)

TIME NEEDED: 15 minutes

Per Serving: Calories 149, Total Fat 4gr (Sat 1g, Mono 2g, Poly 1g) Cholesterol 94mg, Sodium 77mg, Carbs 27g, Fiber 4g, Protein 10g.

Berry Syrup

Pampers the sweet tooth AND guards the waistline.

Makes 2 servings

1 cup mashed strawberries or blueberries, fresh or frozen

2 teaspoons tapioca granules

(Note: Pearl-type tapioca will be too large. It should be the crushed, quicker cooking variety.)

2 to 6 drops stevia (to taste)

½ cup water

Combine all ingredients and bring to a boil over medium heat in a saucepan. Stir constantly until thickened, about five minutes. Serve warm over French toast, pancakes or waffles. Cooled to room temperature, it also makes a nice swirl in plain nonfat yogurt.

TIME NEEDED: 10 minutes

Per Serving: Calories 49, Total Fat 0gr (Sat 0g, Mono 0g, Poly 0g) Cholesterol 0mg, Sodium 1mg, Carbs 12g, Fiber 3g, Protein 1g.

Fiesta Scramble

Festive is the key word. Take scrambled eggs to a new level. A great breakfast for warding off low blood sugar.

Makes 2 servings

1 chopped small onion

½ chopped green pepper

1 teaspoon olive oil

2 eggs

4 egg whites

1 tablespoon water

¼ teaspoon salt (or salt substitute to taste)

¼ teaspoon pepper

3 tablespoons salsa

(Try making your own – see recipe on p.149)

Sauté onion and green pepper in olive oil in a non-stick skillet over medium-high heat for about five minutes. Lightly beat eggs, egg whites, water, salt and pepper. Pour into skillet over onions and peppers and continue to cook, stirring, until eggs are set, about 3-5 minutes. Serve with salsa.

TIME NEEDED: 15 minutes

Per Serving: Calories 155, Total Fat 6gr (Sat 2g, Mono 3g, Poly 1g) Protein 14g.

37

Whole Wheat Waffles with Berry Syrup

These could just as easily be called Heart Healthy Waffles.

Makes 2 servings

½ cup unsweetened applesauce

1 egg white

½ teaspoon vanilla

1 tablespoon olive, almond or hazelnut oil

1 cup nonfat milk or water

1 teaspoon baking powder

1½ cups whole wheat flour

Put all the ingredients into a blender or food processor, except for the baking powder and flour. Blend until well mixed. Combine flour and baking powder. With the blender running, add the flour mixture a little at a time. Blend only until smooth. Cook on a medium-hot waffle iron, sprayed with olive oil spray. These waffles are naturally sweet and crunchy. Serve with Berry Syrup (recipe on page 36).

Variations: If you do desire additional sweetening, use a little brown rice syrup. For another topping option, you could add a few drops of xylitol or stevia to unsweetened applesauce or other fruit.

TIME NEEDED: 15 minutes

Per Serving: Calories 446, Total Fat 7gr (Sat 1g, Mono 5g, Poly 1g) Cholesterol 2mg, Sodium 340mg, Carbs 79g, Fiber 12g, Protein 18g.

Zucchini And Mushroom Frittata

Who said veggies don't have a place in the breakfast menu?

Makes 2 servings

½ chopped yellow onion
1 quartered and sliced zucchini
4 ounces sliced fresh mushrooms
½ chopped green pepper
¼ teaspoon salt
¼ teaspoon pepper
1 teaspoon olive oil
1 tablespoon minced fresh basil
(or ½ teaspoon dried), to taste
2 eggs
4 egg whites

In a nonstick skillet, sauté the onion, zucchini, mushrooms, and green pepper in the olive oil over medium heat. Add the seasonings and basil. Beat the eggs and egg whites with a fork and pour over the vegetable mixture. Cook until the eggs are set but still moist. You can lift the edge away from the pan so that uncooked egg can run under and cook faster. Cover briefly, and when most of the egg is set, place it under the broiler for just a few minutes to lightly brown the top. Good served with wedges of fresh tomato.

TIME NEEDED: 15 minutes

Per Serving: Calories 170, Total Fat 6gr (Sat 2g, Mono 3g, Poly 1g) Cholesterol 187mg, Sodium 117mg, Carbs 12g, Fiber 3g, Protein 16g.

ASK THE DOCTOR

"Our household has pretty much been scared off eggs. Have we been sold a bill of goods with all the negative flap there is about them?"

Eggs are no longer the villains they were once cracked up to be. A 1999 study involving more than 100,000 men and women found that, contrary to popular belief, eating up to seven eggs a week does not increase risk of heart attack. Eggs are a good source of protein, brain-nurturing choline, and antioxidant-rich carotenoids. If you want more than seven eggs a week, stick with egg whites, which are pure protein. (Note: If you have diabetes, go easy on eggs, for they do raise the risk of heart attack in diabetics.)

Western Tofu Scramble

You might expect something weird, but it's surprisingly good. A new taste experience that you're going to want to repeat!

Makes 2 servings
½ cup chopped onion
½ chopped green pepper
1 teaspoon extra-virgin olive oil
1 diced tomato
½ cup sliced mushrooms
8 ounces firm tofu
1 teaspoon onion powder
2 tablespoons grated Parmesan cheese
black pepper, optional

Sauté onion and green pepper in olive oil until tender-crisp. Add tomato and mushrooms and continue cooking for 2 to 3 minutes. Crumble tofu and add to vegetables with the onion powder and blend well. Continue cooking for another 2 to 3 minutes. The cheese can be added during the final minutes of cooking or sprinkled on as a garnish. Note: Use additional salt with discretion, as the cheese already contains a fair amount.

TIME NEEDED: 20 minutes

✳ Cook's Notes: Unless you're making a pudding or beverage, use only firm or extra-firm tofu. It's much easier to handle and retains its shape during cooking.

Per Serving: Calories 174, Total Fat 8gr (Sat 2g, Mono 3g, Poly 3g) Cholesterol 4mg, Sodium 111mg, Carbs 13g, Fiber 3g, Protein 13g.

Greek Omelet

Feta cheese adds a depth that's as intense as the Aegean sun.

Makes 2 servings
½ cup chopped onion
Olive oil spray
¾ cup chopped ripe tomato
4 egg whites
2 whole eggs
2 teaspoons water
Salt substitute, if needed
Dash pepper
4 teaspoons crumbled feta cheese

Sauté onion in preheated medium nonstick skillet with olive oil spray until tender. Add tomato and cook another 2 to 3 minutes. Set vegetables aside and keep warm. Mix eggs with water, salt, and pepper and beat lightly. Re-spray skillet with olive oil, and pour in egg mixture. Cook until eggs begin to set. Turn omelet. Sprinkle vegetables and feta cheese on one half. Cook a touch more until completely set. Fold in half to cover vegetables and cheese. Cook another minute or two, and then slide from pan onto a serving plate.

TIME NEEDED: 15 minutes

Per Serving: Calories 165, Total Fat 8gr (Sat 3g, Mono 4g, Poly 1g) Cholesterol 193mg, Sodium 242mg, Carbs 8g, Fiber 1g, Protein 14g.

THE DOCTOR IS IN:

As you know, cheese contains a lot of saturated fat, which increases the risk of heart disease. This is why I recommend you use strong-flavored cheeses like feta — a little bit goes a long way.

Eggs Florentine

Traditional favorites can be improved to fit into a health-supporting cuisine. Here's proof.

Makes 2 servings

*2 English muffins (sprouted or
whole grain preferred), lightly toasted
1 cup cooked spinach (fresh preferred)
4 poached eggs
4 tablespoons nonfat or low-fat sour cream
Salt and pepper to taste*

On each English muffin half, spread 1/4 cup spinach. Place one egg on each muffin half and top with 1 tablespoon sour cream. Add salt and pepper to taste.

TIME NEEDED: 15 minutes

✳ Cook's Notes: If you don't know how to poach an egg, it's time you learn, for this is one of the healthiest and easiest ways to cook eggs. Bring 1 1/2 inches of water to boil in a medium non-stick skillet. Add 2 tablespoons white vinegar. Break each egg onto a shallow saucer. Gently tip egg from saucer into boiling water. Repeat with additional eggs. Cook until whites are set, about two minutes. Very gently remove eggs with a slotted spoon.

Per Serving: Calories 301, Total Fat 7gr (Sat 3g, Mono 3g, Poly 1g) Cholesterol 377mg, Sodium 380mg, Carbs 34g, Fiber 6g, Protein 22g.

45

Broken Yolk And Bacon Sandwich

A new flip on an over-easy standard.

Makes 2 servings

*2 strips turkey or vegetarian bacon
Olive oil pan spray
2 eggs
4 slices bread, lightly toasted
(sprouted or whole grain preferred)*

Cook bacon in microwave until crisp, about three minutes. Heat nonstick skillet over medium heat. Spray with olive oil pan spray. Add eggs to pan, break yolks, and cook until set, turning once. For each sandwich, use 2 slices of bread, 1 egg, and 1 strip of bacon cut in half.

TIME NEEDED: 10 minutes

✳ Cook's Notes: Vegetarian bacon, which you'll find in your health food store, isn't as scary as it sounds. Granted, it's not a dead ringer for the real thing, but sprinkled over a salad, added to scrambled eggs, or eaten in a BLT or egg sandwich, it's quite good – and it contains no saturated fat or nitrates.

Per Serving: Calories 257, Total Fat 12gr (Sat 3g, Mono 5g, Poly 2g) Cholesterol 199mg, Sodium 535mg, Carbs 27g, Fiber 4g, Protein 13g.

Fruit Sunrise

The bright fruit palette will open your eyes and the great balance of carbs and protein will keep them open. You'll wonder where all the energy came from.

Makes 2 servings
1 apple or pear, cored and cubed
1 cup berries (strawberries, blueberries or raspberries)
1 cup plain nonfat yogurt
1 tablespoon xylitol or
2 to 3 drops stevia (or to taste)
½ cup fat-free granola

Place mixed fruit in individual serving bowls. Stir sweetener into yogurt and put ⅓ cup on top of fruit in each bowl. Top with granola. Other fruit may be substituted; use about 2 cups fruit total.

TIME NEEDED: 10 minutes

Per Serving: Calories 190, Total Fat 1gr (Sat 1g, Mono tr, Poly tr) Cholesterol 2mg, Sodium 101mg, Carbs 39g, Fiber 5g, Protein 8g.

THE DOCTOR IS IN:

The "live and active cultures" in high-quality yogurt help replenish the beneficial bacteria in your intestines. These bacteria manufacture B vitamins, keep pathogens under control, and aid in the digestion and absorption of food.

Cinnamon Poached Fruit with Vanilla Cream

Poaching is an easy, tasty way to dress up fruit.

Makes 4 servings
3 cups coarsely chopped firm pears, tart apples, or a mixture (use Granny Smith, Fuji, or other tart apples)
½ cup water
½ teaspoon cinnamon
2 tablespoons xylitol or 3-4 drops stevia (to taste)
¼ cup chopped walnuts or pecans

Place chopped fruit, water, cinnamon, and sweetener in a medium saucepan. Bring to a boil over medium heat. Cook for 15 minutes, stirring often, until fruit is tender. Serve with 2 tablespoons Vanilla Cream (recipe follows on page 48) and top with 1 scant tablespoon chopped nuts.

TIME NEEDED: 10 minutes

Per Serving: Calories 122, Total Fat 5gr (Sat tr, Mono 1g, Poly 3g) Cholesterol 0mg, Sodium 0mg, Carbs 20g, Fiber 4g, Protein 2g.

Vanilla Cream

When you're craving something sweet and creamy, you've got to have sweet and creamy.

Makes 2 cups

1 pint nonfat cottage cheese
1 to 2 tablespoons nonfat milk
1 teaspoon vanilla
2 to 3 drops stevia (or more to taste)

Place cottage cheese, 1 tablespoon milk, vanilla, and 2 drops stevia in blender or food processor. Process until smooth. If needed, add more milk to achieve a thick, creamy texture. You may also add more stevia for a sweeter taste. Serve over Cinnamon Poached Fruit, 2 tablespoons per serving. Vanilla Cream keeps well in the refrigerator.

TIME NEEDED: 5 minutes

Per 1/2 cup: Calories 76, Total Fat tr (Sat tr, Mono tr, Poly tr) Cholesterol 5mg, Sodium 303mg, Carbs 4g, Fiber 0g, Protein 15g.

Winter Warm-Up Cereal with Stewed Apricots

Stoke your furnace before you set foot out the door on those bone-chilling mornings.

Makes 3 servings

1 cup old-fashioned rolled oats (not instant) or whole multi-grain cereal
2 to 3 cups water (as directed)
½ cup mixed pumpkin seeds, sunflower seeds, and toasted slivered almonds.

Bring water to a boil over medium high heat. Stir in oatmeal or multigrain cereal, cover, lower heat, and simmer until done (oatmeal takes 5 minutes; multigrain about 15 minutes). Stir in nuts and seeds when done. Serve with Stewed Apricots (recipe follows on page 49).

TIME NEEDED: No more than 15 minutes

Per Serving: Calories 245, Total Fat 14gr (Sat 1g, Mono 9g, Poly 3g) Cholesterol 0mg, Sodium 3mg, Carbs 23g, Fiber 4g, Protein 9g.

THE DOCTOR IS IN:

Apricots are an excellent source of vitamin A, and dried apricots are a particularly concentrated source of this vital nutrient. Another good thing about dried apricots is that they have a much lower glycemic rating than dates, raisins and other dried fruits.

Stewed Apricots

This sweet concoction also makes a great dessert or yogurt topping.

Makes 3 servings

1 cup dried coarsely chopped apricots
(sulfite-free preferred)
¼ teaspoon cinnamon
2 to 3 drops stevia (to taste)
1 cup water

Place chopped apricots, cinnamon and stevia in medium saucepan and cover with water.
Bring to a boil over medium heat, then reduce heat to low, cover and gently simmer 20 to 30 minutes until apricots are tender. Serve over Winter Warm-Up Cereal.

TIME NEEDED: 5 minutes preparation, plus cooking

Per Serving: Calories 104, Total Fat 0gr (Sat 0g, Mono 0g, Poly 0g) Cholesterol 0mg, Sodium 4mg, Carbs 27g, Fiber 4g, Protein 2g.

Spicy Sweet Potato Hash Browns

Asians consider the sweet potato to be one of the most nutritious of all vegetables, and with good reason – the payload of vitamins, minerals, and fiber is awesome!

Makes 4 servings

1 ½ pounds sweet potatoes*, peeled and
cut into ½ -inch pieces
1 teaspoon paprika
1 teaspoon chili powder
1 teaspoon cayenne, Creole, or Cajun seasoning
¼ teaspoon salt
¼ cup olive oil

Preheat oven to 400°F. Sprinkle spices over potato pieces in large bowl and stir or toss to mix well. Add olive oil in small amounts and stir well so potatoes are evenly coated. Spread potatoes on large baking sheet and bake for 45 minutes until crisp, turning with spatula every 10 minutes while cooking.

TIME NEEDED: 10 minutes preparation, plus 45 minutes baking time

✳ Cook's Notes: What's the difference between yams and sweet potatoes? Although they are technically two different species, many of the yams sold in this country are actually sweet potatoes and vice-versa. Bright-orange, moist-fleshed, darker-skinned varieties are referred to as yams, while the paler, drier ones are called sweet potatoes.

Per Serving: Calories 336, Total Fat 14gr (Sat 2g, Mono 10g, Poly 1g) Cholesterol 0mg, Sodium 160mg, Carbs 30, Fiber 6g, Protein 3g.

Sunshine Muffins

Cranberries only on Thanksgiving? These rubies in the rough deserve more of the limelight and this recipe gives them their proper due.

Makes 12 muffins

Olive oil spray

1¾ cups whole wheat flour

⅓ cup chopped pecans

½ cup xylitol

2 teaspoons baking power

½ teaspoon baking soda

¼ teaspoon salt or salt substitute

¼ teaspoon nutmeg

1 egg

¾ cup nonfat milk

½ cup orange juice

⅓ cup hazelnut, almond, or olive oil

2 to 4 tablespoons coarsely chopped, unsweetened cranberries

2 tablespoons brown rice syrup, optional

Multi-grain flakes, optional for garnishing

Preheat oven to 400° F. Spray muffin pan with olive oil spray (or use paper baking cups). Combine flour, nuts, xylitol, baking powder, baking soda, salt, and nutmeg in a large mixing bowl and stir until well blended. Combine egg, milk, orange juice, and oil in a small mixing bowl and stir well. Add the liquid and cranberries into dry ingredients and stir just until moistened. (Batter will be lumpy.) Spoon into prepared muffin pan, filling each cup about ²/₃ full. Bake for 20 minutes, or until golden brown and muffins spring back when lightly touched. If desired, drizzle on brown rice syrup to hold on multi-grain flakes.

TIME NEEDED: 45 minutes

Per Muffin: Calories 178, Total Fat 9gr (Sat 1g, Mono 6g, Poly 1g) Cholesterol 16mg, Sodium 148mg, Carbs 22g, Fiber 2g, Protein 4g.

51

ASK THE DOCTOR

"I've just been diagnosed with diabetes and I'm trying to avoid sugar. What do you recommend?"

I suggest you try xylitol, a sweetener derived from birch trees. Although it is not calorie-free, xylitol is very slowly metabolized, so it does not cause sharp rises and falls in blood sugar, making it ideal for diabetics. Because xylitol looks and tastes like sugar, it is particularly useful in baking and can be substituted for sugar in most recipes.

Xylitol has other health benefits as well. It protects the teeth and gums by inhibiting the growth of *Streptococcus mutans*, the leading culprit in tooth decay. Whereas sugar is *S. mutans'* favorite food, this bacteria is unable to metabolize xylitol. Xylitol also raises the pH of the mouth, making it less hospitable to *S. mutans*, and over time, these microorganisms are crowded out by harmless bacteria. Xylitol has also been shown to inhibit the growth of bacteria that cause ear infections in young children. In recent studies, xylitol-flavored chewing gum reduced the incidence of ear infections by 40 percent, significantly decreasing the need for antibiotics.

Berry-Banana Smoothie

For breakfast on the run, nothing beats a smoothie.

Makes 2 servings

1 cup frozen berries* (of your choice)

1 banana, barely ripe

¼ cup flaxseed, freshly ground

2 scoops protein powder

½ cup nonfat yogurt (optional)

1 cup soy milk (or water)

1 cup ice

*Fresh berries may be purchased, but should be frozen before making the drink. Mix all ingredients in blender and blend until smooth. Adjust soy milk and ice to obtain desired thickness. This is a delightful, well-balanced, and nutritious meal replacement. Use your imagination and substitute the berries and bananas with other fruits in season for a rich supply of nutrients.

TIME NEEDED: 5 minutes

Per Serving: Calories 290, Total Fat 11gr (Sat 1g, Mono 3g, Poly 6g) Cholesterol 1mg, Sodium 67mg, Carbs 38g, Fiber 11g, Protein 16g.

THE DOCTOR IS IN:

I am a big fan of smoothies for breakfast. As this recipe attests, you can pack a powerhouse of nutrition into a glass – and drink it on the go! If you aren't a regular breakfast eater, get into the habit of making a smoothie every morning.

Orange Julian

You can have it two ways – as a breakfast smoothie or a hearty between-meals snack.

Makes 2 servings

2 large oranges, juiced
1 cup nonfat yogurt or buttermilk
1 tablespoon xylitol or stevia to taste
1 cup ice

Pour juice and other ingredients into a blender, and blend until ice is crushed. Add a little water, if you like a thinner drink. For an occasional treat, substitute nonfat yogurt with low-fat or fat-free ice cream. *Optional garnish:* Skewered pieces of orange and banana.

TIME NEEDED: 5 minutes

Per Serving: Calories 133, Total Fat tr (Sat tr, Mono tr, Poly tr) Cholesterol 2mg, Sodium 87mg, Carbs 26g, Fiber 3g, Protein 8g.

Papaya-Lime Smoothie

Stretch your taste experience with this simple but dynamite combination.

Makes 2 servings

½ lime, juiced
2 cups cubed papaya
1 cup plain nonfat yogurt
1 cup ice
1 tablespoon protein powder
Stevia for sweetening if needed

Place all ingredients except stevia in blender. Blend until smooth. Taste and add sweetener if desired.

TIME NEEDED: 10 minutes

Per Serving: Calories 131, Total Fat 1gr (Sat tr, Mono tr, Poly tr) Cholesterol 2mg, Sodium 119mg, Carbs 24g, Fiber 3g, Protein 9g.

55

THE DOCTOR IS IN:

For extra fiber, protein and heart-healthy omega-3 fatty acids, add up to ¼ cup freshly ground flaxseed to any smoothie. Sunflower seeds also make a great garnish and add a nice crunch.

Midday Meals

If you've eaten slow-burning carbohydrates and moderate amounts of protein and healthy fats for breakfast, as suggested in the Start Your Day recipes, you've likely made it through the morning without a let down. Starting your day with proper nutrition brings quick payoff. You won't have the mid-morning drop in blood sugar that can leave you tired, irritable, and ravenously hungry.

Now the trick with lunch is to add more of the same power-packed fuel to your tank, nutrients that will keep you on a roll through the entire afternoon. With any of these lunches, it should be smooth sailing until dinner.

s o u p s

Soup can, of course, be served as a first course to a formal meal. However, most of the recipes in this section are hearty enough to build a meal around. Some contain fiber-rich barley, lentils, or beans, which guarantee a full belly that's not going to growl before it's time for the next meal. Others provide a cornucopia of vegetables and health-enhancing vitamins, minerals, and phytonutrients. One thing they all have in common is ease of preparation and great taste.

Miso Soup

This soup has appeared on the Japanese table for centuries – it certainly plays a role in Japan's low rate of heart disease. It's amazing that a soup with so few calories can pack so much flavor. Once you buy miso for this soup, it's sure to find its way into other dishes as well.

Makes 2 servings

3 cups low-sodium vegetable or chicken stock
½ cup onions, thinly sliced
½ cup firm tofu, cut into ¼ inch cubes
3 tablespoons miso paste
1 tablespoon chopped green onions

Heat stock in medium saucepan. Add onions and simmer for 5 minutes. Then add tofu and simmer 1-2 minutes longer. In a cup or small bowl, mix miso with 2 tablespoons of the broth and add back to soup. Heat for another minute. Garnish with green onions and serve.

TIME NEEDED: 15 minutes

Per Serving: Calories 145, Total fat 4g (Sat fat 1g/ Mono fat 1g/ Poly fat 2 g) Cholesterol 0mg, Sodium 943mg, Carbs 16g, Fiber 3g, Protein 25g.

✳ Cook's Notes: Miso is a Japanese staple made of fermented rice or soybeans and is sold in health food stores and Asian markets. It is richly flavored and very nutritious. It also contains a lot of sodium, so if you are sodium sensitive, replace some of the broth or stock with water and cut miso paste back to 2 tablespoons.

Spicy Split Pea Soup

It will stick to your ribs, but not your waistline. Split peas are on a par with beans, fiberwise – unbeatable.

Makes 3 servings
1 cup uncooked split peas
5 cups low-sodium vegetable or chicken stock
1 cup chopped onion
3 tablespoons salsa

Wash peas under running water. Mix all ingredients except for salsa in a stockpot. Bring to a boil, and simmer until the peas are tender (about one hour). Stir occasionally and add more water as needed. Top each serving with 1 tablespoon salsa.

TIME NEEDED: 1 hour

✳ Cook's Notes: Make soup in volume – double or triple the recipe. Then enjoy the leftovers in a day or two, or freeze individual-sized servings.

Per Serving: Calories 277, Total fat 1g (Sat fat trace/ Mono fat trace/ Poly fat trace) Cholesterol 0mg, Sodium 914mg, Carbs 48g, Fiber 18g, Protein 35g.

Broccoli Cheddar Soup

Broccoli is a vitamin and mineral storehouse with superior cancer-preventing power. Make the effort to develop a taste for it and search out new ways to make it a regular on your table.

Makes 6 servings
4 cups fresh chopped broccoli
½ cup chopped onion
2 tablespoons cornstarch
3 cups nonfat milk (divided use)
½ cup low-fat grated sharp cheddar cheese
Salt and pepper to taste

Place broccoli and onion in medium saucepan and cover with water. Bring to a boil and cook just until tender, about 7 to 10 minutes. Drain and place broccoli in blender or food processor, along with 1 cup of the milk, and blend just until smooth. In the same saucepan, stir cornstarch into 2 cups of milk. Bring slowly to a boil over medium heat, stirring constantly until mixture has boiled about 1 minute. Add broccoli mixture to saucepan and heat to serving temperature. Stir in cheese until it's melted. Salt and pepper to taste.

TIME NEEDED: 30 minutes

Per Serving: Calories 91, Total fat 1g (Sat fat 1g/ Mono fat trace/ Poly fat trace) Cholesterol 4mg, Sodium 236mg, Carbs 22g, Fiber 3g, Protein 8g.

THE DOCTOR IS IN:

Don't like broccoli? Maybe you're a "supertaster." About a quarter of the population has been identified as having this genetic variation: they simply have more taste buds than "nontasters" (25 percent of the population) or medium tasters (50 percent). If you find broccoli, cabbage, and coffee very bitter - and sweets supersweet – consider yourself a supertaster. Even so you'll probably like the recipe above. The milk and cheese take the edge off the broccoli.

62

Versatile Cream Of Vegetable Soup

You don't need cream or high-fat milk to achieve a rich, creamy soup.

Makes 4 servings

2 medium chopped carrots
2 medium chopped onions
1 small chopped green pepper
3 chopped zucchini
3 stalks chopped celery
½ cup chopped parsley
1 teaspoon onion powder
½ teaspoon seasoned salt or salt substitute
½ teaspoon pepper
2 cups nonfat milk

In a medium saucepan, cover vegetables and fresh parsley with water and simmer over medium heat until the carrots are tender. Drain, then puree vegetables in blender or food processor until creamy, adding seasonings and milk as needed. When smooth, add remaining milk and return to saucepan and heat to serving temperature. (For a thinner soup, add more milk.)

TIME NEEDED: 30 minutes

✳ Cook's Notes: The water that you drain off the boiled vegetables doesn't need to be discarded. Cool this nutrient-rich broth and freeze it for a different soup you make later. Soups are a wonderful way to clean out the refrigerator, and this recipe is a perfect example. It works with any combination of vegetables, fresh or frozen.

Per Serving: Calories 108, Total fat 1g (Sat fat trace/ Mono fat trace/ Poly fat trace) Cholesterol 1mg, Sodium 282mg, Carbs 21g, Fiber 5g, Protein 7g.

VARIATIONS: Add any of the following to the recipe above before cooking and enjoy four different soups:

Spinach: 1 package thawed frozen spinach or 1 pound chopped fresh spinach, cleaned and stemmed, and 1 clove minced or pressed garlic

Mushroom: 2 cups chopped mushrooms and ½ teaspoon thyme

Peas: 1½ cups fresh or thawed frozen peas, ½ teaspoon marjoram and ½ teaspoon thyme

Tomato: 1 cup tomato puree and 1 clove minced or pressed garlic

Hearty Lentil Kale Stew

The great thing about lentils is that they pack the same protein and fiber wallop as beans, but they cook in about 30 minutes

Makes 3-4 servings

1 large diced onion

2 cloves minced garlic

Olive oil pan spray

5 cups low-sodium, nonfat vegetable or chicken stock

1 sliced carrot

¾ cup lentils, rinsed

14-ounce can tomatoes with juice, finely chopped (buy low-sodium tomatoes if possible)

1 bunch kale, washed and coarsely chopped

Spray the bottom of a large stockpot with olive oil and sauté onions and garlic for ten minutes over medium heat. Add remaining ingredients and bring to a boil. Reduce heat and simmer, stirring occasionally. Serve as soon as the lentils are tender, about 30 minutes.

TIME NEEDED: 45 minutes

Per Serving: Calories 215; Total fat 2g (Sat fat 0g/ Mono fat 1g/ Poly fat 1g) Cholesterol 0mg, Sodium 693mg, Carbs 37g, Fiber 14g, Protein 27g.

THE DOCTOR IS IN:

Kale, spinach, and other dark leafy greens are nature's best sources of lutein and zeaxanthin. These phytonutrients filter light as it enters the eye and absorb damaging radiation. A recent study found that eating lots of these vegetables lowered the risk of macular degeneration (the leading cause of blindness in people over age 50) by 43 percent.

(Not Your Average) Mushroom Barley Medley

Have a recipe card handy, because this is one of those you'll want to pass on to a friend.
Healthy, creamy, and hearty – all in one bowl. Smooth sailing until dinner.

Makes 8 to 10 servings

16 oz. mixed chopped mushrooms
(button, shiitake, cremini, oyster, enoki, etc.)
2 portobello mushrooms
Olive oil spray
2 chopped large onions
2 minced cloves garlic
2 cups turnip cubes, ½-inch dice
1 teaspoon dried or 1 tablespoon fresh thyme
¼ teaspoon salt or salt substitute
4 cups non-fat or low-fat cream of mushroom soup
4 cups low sodium French onion soup (without cheese!)
⅓ cup pearl barley

After removing all mushroom stems, wash and chop mushroom caps. Spray a large stock pot with olive oil and heat over medium-high heat for one minute. Add onions, garlic, turnip, and thyme, and sauté over medium heat until onions are golden brown. Add mushrooms and salt and reduce heat to low. Stir mixture for 20 to 30 minutes until almost all the liquid is evaporated. Add both soups and the barley, heat to a boil, then reduce heat, cover and simmer. The soup is ready when the barley is as soft as you like it. Forty minutes is usually adequate. Feel free to add stock or water to control the thickness of the soup.

TIME NEEDED: 20 minutes preparation, 1½ hours from start to finish.

Per Serving: Calories 145, Total fat 3g (Sat fat 1g/ Mono fat 1g/ Poly fat 1g) Cholesterol 9mg, Sodium 527mg, Carbs 22g, Fiber 3g, Protein 8g.

67

THE DOCTOR IS IN:

Barley is one of the world's most digestible grains. Archeological discoveries suggest it has been cultivated for more than 8,000 years. This nutrient-dense grain is a particularly rich source of soluble fiber and beta-glucan, which, in addition to lowering cholesterol, supports the immune system.

Cuban Black Bean Soup

Other kinds of dried beans can be substituted, but the texture, color, and flavor of the soup will be slightly different. Cooking time may also vary.

Makes 6 generous servings

1¼ cups black beans

1½ quarts water

1 cup chopped onion

½ cup chopped celery

½ cup chopped carrot

1 bay leaf

3 whole cloves

¼ teaspoon crushed red pepper

2 teaspoons vinegar

½ cup medium sherry

Salt to taste

1 chopped hard-boiled egg

2 chopped green onions

Soak beans overnight according to package directions. Drain. Put beans, water, onion, celery, carrot, bay leaf, cloves and red pepper in a large stockpot. Bring to a boil and skim off foam. Reduce heat and simmer 4 hours, adding a little more water as needed. Once the beans are tender, add vinegar, sherry, and salt. Cook another 30 minutes. Garnish with chopped egg and chopped green onion.

TIME NEEDED: 30 minutes for preparation, 4½ hours cooking time.

Per Serving: Calories 194, Total fat 1g (Sat fat tr/ Mono fat tr/ Poly fat tr) Cholesterol 31mg, Sodium 204mg, Carbs 31g, Fiber 7g, Protein 10g.

68

ASK THE DOCTOR

"I love beans, but they don't like me, if you know what I mean. Any suggestions?"

I share your infatuation with beans. Not only are beans tasty and versatile, they are also low in fat, high in protein and minerals, and one of our best sources of cholesterol-lowering soluble fiber.

Now, about the dark side of beans: Blame it on oligosaccharides, sugar molecules that are particularly abundant in beans but are also found in cabbage and other "gassy" foods. Human beings do not produce the enzyme that breaks down these sugars. Therefore, as these sugars arrive intact in the intestinal tract, the trillions of bacteria that reside in the gut have a field day. Bacteria metabolize sugars in a fermentation process and the byproduct of fermentation, as you know, is gas.

There are a few ways to cut down on gas. Soaking and rinsing beans well before cooking helps a lot. Baking soda may also help. Place beans in a large saucepan and cover with several inches of water. Add one teaspoon baking soda, boil for ten minutes, then soak at room temperature overnight. Always discard soaking water, rinse, and cover with new water before cooking.

You can also try Beano from AkPharma. This product contains an enzyme that breaks down oligosaccharides into digestible sugars.

s a l a d s

If your idea of salad is iceberg lettuce, chopped tomatoes, and bottled salad dressing, you're in for a treat. The salads in this section contain everything from whole grains like bulgur and brown rice to chicken and salmon. In fact, many are hearty enough to serve as a main course.

Lebanese Tabouli

This is a very satisfying meal all by itself. Look for bulgur wheat in the ethnic section of your grocery store.

Makes 6 servings

3 cups water

1¼ cups uncooked bulgur

3 chopped scallions

1 cup minced fresh parsley

3 tomatoes, peeled and finely chopped

Juice of two lemons

¼ cup extra-virgin olive oil

Salt or salt substitute to taste

Crisp chilled lettuce

Tomato wedges

1 slice Bermuda onion, cut in half

Bring water to a boil and pour over bulgur. Let it stand for 1 hour or until grain is light and fluffy. Press out excess water through a strainer. Place in a bowl and mix with scallions, parsley, chopped tomatoes, lemon juice, olive oil, and salt. Chill several hours before serving. Serve on a bed of crisp chilled lettuce and garnish with tomato wedges and sliced onion.

Chilling time needed, plus 1½ hours for preparation

✳ Cook's Notes: Bulgur is whole wheat that has been cooked, dried, and ground. Look for it in ethnic shops or the bins of your health food store. If you can't find bulgur, substitute cracked wheat. (Because it hasn't been precooked, it may require more soaking or cooking and will have a chewier texture.)

Per Serving: Calories 203, Total fat 10g (Sat fat 1g/ Mono fat 7g/ Poly fat 1g) Cholesterol 0mg, Sodium 22mg, Carbs 28g, Fiber 7g, Protein 5g.

Salad Caprese

Got home from work late and your stomach is growling louder than the neighbor's dog? Company shows up unexpectedly and you need something fast with flair? Great taste, nutrition, and ease.

Makes 2 servings

2 large tomatoes, sliced

2 thin slices mozzarella cheese

10 large fresh basil leaves

1 teaspoon balsamic vinegar

2 teaspoons extra virgin olive oil

Place the tomato, cheese, and basil on salad plates. Combine vinegar and oil and stir well. Sprinkle salads with dressing.

TIME NEEDED: 10 minutes max!

❉ Cook's Notes: Fresh basil is such a delightful herb that you might want to grow it yourself. Basil doesn't require much tending and takes up little space. Young plants, which you'll find in your local nursery in the spring, can be tucked into a corner of your yard or grown in containers. A couple of plants will easily provide a summer of Salad Caprese, pesto, and other basil-inspired dishes.

Per Serving: Calories 157, Total fat 12g (Sat fat 5g/ Mono fat 5g/ Poly fat 2g) Cholesterol 25mg, Sodium 129mg, Carbs 7g, Fiber 1g, Protein 7g.

74

Spicy Sesame Cucumber Salad

This recipe retains its vibrant flavor when made in small batches and eaten soon after marinating.

Makes 4 servings

2 medium cucumbers

1 teaspoon soy sauce

1 tablespoon rice wine vinegar

1 tablespoon xylitol

2 teaspoons toasted sesame seed oil

¼ teaspoon Tabasco or hot sauce

½ teaspoon salt

Peel cucumbers, and cut in half lengthwise. Scoop out seeds with a spoon, then slice cucumbers into ¼-inch slices and set aside. Combine all other ingredients in a shallow bowl, and stir well. Add cucumber slices to dressing and toss to make sure each slice is coated. Cover and marinate in refrigerator for about 3 hours, occasionally shaking bowl to redistribute dressing.

TIME NEEDED: 10 minutes preparation, plus 3 hours for marinating.

❉ Cook's Notes: Peeling cucumbers is optional – unless they've been waxed, which seems to be the rule, rather than the exception. Pesticides are often trapped under these waxes, which are applied to prevent produce from drying out, and they are nearly impossible to scrub off.

Per Serving: Calories 53; Total fat 2g (Sat fat 1g/ Mono fat 1g/ Poly fat 0g) Cholesterol 0mg, Sodium 355mg, Carbs 8g, Fiber 1g, Protein 1g.

Salad Niçoise

Niçoise is to France what coleslaw is to America.

Makes 2 servings

1 cup sliced cooked new red potatoes
1 cup green beans cooked al dente
1 head butter lettuce
2 medium quartered tomatoes
1 small can water-packed tuna,
drained and chunked
4 anchovies (optional)
1 hardboiled egg, cut in quarters
6 black olives (Niçoise preferred)

Mix potatoes and green beans with half of the Basil Dressing. (See recipe below.) Toss and chill several hours. Line bowls with lettuce leaves. Mound potato-bean mixture in center of each bowl. Place remaining ingredients around potatoes and beans, and then top with dressing.

TIME NEEDED: 35 minutes

✳ Cook's Notes: The Niçoise in Niçoise Salad comes from the olives native to the Nice area in Southern France. Using these small, tender, rosy-tinted olives (they're marinated in red wine vinegar) is not crucial, but they do make this French salad more authentic. You'll find Niçoise olives in gourmet shops and delis.

Per Serving: Calories 267, Total fat 6g (Sat fat 1g/ Mono fat 3g/ Poly fat 2g) Cholesterol 123mg, Sodium 719mg, Carbs 26g, Fiber 6g, Protein 29g.

75

Basil Dressing

Fresh herbs spruce up this simple oil and vinegar dressing.

Makes 2 servings

2 tablespoons extra-virgin olive oil
2 tablespoons red wine vinegar
1 tablespoon chopped parsley
2 teaspoons chopped fresh basil
(or 1 teaspoon dried)
¼ teaspoon salt
Dash pepper

Combine ingredients and mix until well blended. Serve with Salad Niçoise.

Per Serving: Calories 126, Total fat 20g (Sat fat 3g/ Mono fat 15g/ Poly fat 2g) Cholesterol 0mg, Sodium 268mg, Carbs 2g, Fiber 1g, Protein trace.

Greek Village Salad

The vivid green, red, black and white will draw you in. The taste will hold you.

Makes 2 servings

1 large sliced cucumber (¼" slices)
1 large tomato chopped into chunks
½ cup black olives
(Kalamata olives preferred)
½ cup crumbled feta cheese
1 small chopped onion (optional)
2 chopped anchovies (optional)
2 small pita rounds (whole grain preferred)

Combine salad ingredients in large bowl. Toss with Herb Vinaigrette (recipe follows) and serve with pita cut in wedges, toasted or untoasted. For variety, can also be prepared as pocket pita sandwiches. To lower sodium content, cut back on anchovies, olives and feta.

❋ Cook's Notes: It's worth the effort to check out gourmet shops and delis for Kalamata olives. Grown in the Kalamata region of Southern Greece and cured for three months in vinegar and olive oil, these almond-shaped, eggplant-colored olives are unsurpassed in flavor.

Per Serving: Calories 364, Total fat 13g (Sat fat 6g/ Mono fat 5g/ Poly fat 2g) Cholesterol 37mg, Sodium 1188mg, Carbs 49g, Fiber 5g, Protein 14g.

Herb Vinaigrette

Just how much is a pinch? If you're herb crazy, put several fingers together.

Makes 2 servings

2 tablespoons extra virgin olive oil
1 tablespoon vinegar
½ teaspoon minced garlic
¼ teaspoon salt
¼ teaspoon black pepper
Pinch of dill (dried dill weed or fresh chopped)
Pinch of rosemary (crushed dry or fresh chopped)
Pinch of oregano (dry or fresh chopped)

Blend ingredients together. Serve with Greek Village Salad. Making the dressing ahead, if time permits, allows the herbs to infuse the dressing more dramatically.

TIME NEEDED: 5 minutes

Per Serving: Calories 123, Total fat 14g (Sat fat 2g/Mono fat 10g/Poly fat 2g) Cholesterol 0mg, Sodium 267mg, Carbs 1g, Fiber trace, Protein trace.

Indian Cucumber Salad (Raita)

Especially good with Indian dishes. The coolness of the yogurt perfectly complements spicy, fiery curries.

Makes 4 servings

16 ounces plain nonfat yogurt
1 peeled, seeded, chopped cucumber
⅛ teaspoon cayenne pepper
½ teaspoon cumin seed
(or ¼ teaspoon ground cumin)
2 tablespoons chopped fresh cilantro
Pinch of salt or salt substitute

Combine all ingredients. Garnish with extra cilantro.

TIME NEEDED: 10 minutes max!

Per Serving: Calories 74, Total fat tr (Sat fat tr/ Mono fat tr/ Poly fat tr) Cholesterol 2mg, Sodium 89mg, Carbs 11g, Fiber 1g, Protein 7g.

Mandarin-Sesame Slaw

A double whammy of sesame adds nutty richness to this fruity slaw.

Makes 2 servings

1½ cup chopped cabbage
½ cup Mandarin orange segments,
chilled and drained
1 tablespoon sesame oil
1 tablespoon toasted sesame seeds

Oranges can be fresh or canned, cut or in whole segments. Mix cabbage and oranges, toss with oil, and sprinkle with sesame seeds.

TIME NEEDED: 10 minutes max!

Per Serving:Calories 124, Total fat 9g (Sat fat 1g/ Mono fat 4g/ Poly fat 4g) Cholesterol 0mg, Sodium 13mg, Carbs 10g, Fiber 3g, Protein 2g.

THE DOCTOR IS IN:

Sesame oil has a long history of culinary and medicinal use. This strong-flavored oil is a favorite in Asian cuisine. It is also used therapeutically in ayurveda, the ancient Indian system of medicine. Rubbing sesame oil into the skin is said to be particularly useful for balancing vata, which is characterized by anxiety, poor circulation, nervousness, and digestive problems.

Field Greens With Balsamic Vinaigrette

The perfect accompaniment for Blackened Salmon Salad, page 81.

Makes 4 servings

½ cup chopped tomatoes
2 tablespoons olive oil
1 tablespoon balsamic vinegar
2 teaspoons Dijon mustard
1 pound washed mixed field greens
1½ tablespoon spice mixture (reserved from Blackened Salmon recipe on page 81) or spices of your choice

In a small bowl, mix the reserved 1½ tablespoons of spice, olive oil, vinegar, and mustard. Toss greens and tomatoes together and divide among 4 serving plates. Place a cooked salmon fillet on top of each plate of greens and then spoon the dressing over both fish and greens, distributing it evenly. Bon appétit!

✳ Cook's Notes: Premixed greens can be purchased or you can simply choose from your favorites. Adding some dark greens like spinach and cilantro will help ensure greater nutrient value and flavor.

Per Serving: Calories 96, Total fat 7g (Sat fat 1g/ Mono fat 5g/ Poly fat 1g) Cholesterol 0mg, Sodium 320mg, Carbs 7g, Fiber 4g, Protein 3g.

Blackened Salmon Salad

Spice-crusted fillets with beautiful black grill marks make this salad as artistic as it is filling.

Makes 4 servings

2 tablespoons chili powder

1 tablespoon garlic powder

1 tablespoon onion powder

3 tablespoons xylitol (or brown sugar)

1 teaspoon salt

¼ teaspoon ground pepper

1 tablespoon paprika

1 tablespoon olive oil or olive oil spray

4 salmon fillets (5 ounce fillets)

Combine chili, garlic, onion, xylitol, salt, pepper, and paprika and mix thoroughly. Reserve 1½ tablespoons of this spice mixture to use in the salad dressing. Rub the rest on all sides of the salmon fillets and marinate for 6 hours. Before cooking, rub or spray fillets with a small amount of olive oil (no more than 1 tablespoon). Preheat broiler or grill until it is very hot. Place salmon on grill/broiler, and cook approximately 7 to 10 minutes, depending on thickness. Place on top of salad with Balsamic Vinaigrette Dressing (see recipe on page 79).

TIME NEEDED: 3 (satisfactory) to 6 (ideal) hours for marinating; 30 minutes preparation.

Per Serving: Calories 224, Total fat 9g (Sat fat 1g/ Mono fat 4g/ Poly fat 4g) Cholesterol 74mg, Sodium 668mg, Carbs 6g, Fiber 2g, Protein 29g.

ASK THE DOCTOR

"What's all the fuss over salmon?"

Like all fish, salmon provides an excellent low-fat source of protein. What sets salmon apart is that it and a handful of other cold-water fish contain omega-3 fatty acids. More than 4,500 studies document the remarkable benefits of eicosapentaenoic acid (EPA) and docosahexaenoic acid (DHA), omega-3 fats found in these fish.

DHA is one of the most abundant fats in the brain, and low levels of this vital nutrient are associated with depression, bipolar disorder, Alzheimer's disease, dementia, and attention deficit disorder. EPA improves circulation, lowers cholesterol and triglyceride levels, protects the arteries by curbing inflammation, and reduces the risk of sudden cardiac death by stabilizing electrical activity in the heart. Eating salmon and other fatty fish regularly dramatically lowers the risk of Alzheimer's and other forms of dementia, as well as risk of death from heart attack.

But the benefits don't stop here. The anti-inflammatory actions of the omega-3 fatty acids make them an effective therapy for rheumatoid arthritis and related conditions. Adequate intake of these oils also improves the cells' sensitivity to insulin, protects against cancer, boosts memory and mood, and even helps with weight loss. I highly recommend that you eat omega-3 rich salmon, trout, sardines, mackerel, herring, and anchovies two or three times a week.

sides &
light entrées

Take a break from the traditional side dishes of potatoes and limp, overcooked vegetables. Expand your horizons beyond lunchmeat sandwiches. Treat your taste buds to these quick and easy side dishes and light entrées from around the world.

Open-Faced Goat Cheese Sandwich

Make today an Alpine picnic, wherever you are.

Makes 2 servings

2 slices sprouted grain bread
2 teaspoons Dijon mustard
½ thinly sliced avocado
2 ounces goat cheese, thinly sliced
½ cup alfalfa sprouts
1 small thinly sliced tomato

Lightly toast bread, trim crusts, and cut each slice into quarters. Spread mustard on the bread slices, then layer as follows: avocado, thin slices of goat cheese, sprouts, and tomato slices.

TIME NEEDED: 10 minutes

Per Serving: Calories 292, Total fat 18g (Sat fat 8g/ Mono fat 8g/ Poly fat 2g) Cholesterol 30mg, Sodium 309mg, Carbs 20g, Fiber 4g, Protein 13g.

THE DOCTOR IS IN:

Although goat's milk cheese is somewhat lower in saturated fat than regular cheeses, it still contains a hefty amount of fat. Goat's milk, however, is more easily digested and better tolerated than cow's milk because it contains smaller, shorter-chained fat molecules. Although two-thirds of the world's population has trouble digesting cow's milk, fewer than 5 percent have problems with goat's milk.

Mediterranean Garbanzo Dip

Since this dip is a variation of the classic hummus, it is best served with fresh or toasted pita wedges. If you opt for chips, choose the organic baked ones.

Makes 6 servings

1 16-ounce can garbanzo beans, rinsed and drained
1 stalk finely diced celery
¼ cup finely diced parsley
1 clove minced garlic
1 teaspoon ground cumin
¼ teaspoon cayenne pepper
1 finely diced tomato

Place garbanzo beans, celery, parsley, garlic and spices into a blender or food processor and process until smooth. Spoon into a serving bowl, add tomatoes, and stir until blended. Serve with pita bread (whole-wheat preferred, toasting optional), cut into triangles.

TIME NEEDED: 20 minutes

Cook's Notes: What's the difference between garbanzo beans and chick peas? Nothing! They're one and the same. Whatever the name, these beans are a good source of soluble fiber, folate, potassium, and other minerals.

Per Serving: Calories 282, Total fat 4g (Sat fat 0g/ Mono fat 2g/ Poly fat 2g) Cholesterol 0mg, Sodium 27mg, Carbs 47g, Fiber 14g, Protein 15g.

Curried Eggs Idel

Tahini is sesame seed butter. Like peanut butter, it is made by finely grinding and blending the seeds. Tahini can be used as a spread, and it is a required ingredient in hummus and other Middle Eastern dishes. It is sold in ethnic shops and health food stores.

Makes 4 servings

4 hard-boiled eggs, halved with yolks removed*

1 cup canned garbanzo beans, drained and rinsed

2 cloves garlic

2 teaspoons olive oil

2 teaspoons tahini

2 teaspoons lemon juice

1 teaspoon curry powder

3 to 4 drops Tabasco sauce (to taste)

3 to 4 sprigs fresh parsley

¼ teaspoon salt

Parsley for garnish

Place beans, garlic, oil, tahini, lemon juice, curry powder, Tabasco, salt and parsley in food processor. Blend until smooth. (*The yolks can also be blended with the other ingredients if you need not worry about cholesterol, heart disease, etc.)

Add this mixture to a pastry bag and pipe into the egg white halves. Garnish with parsley and more curry powder.

TIME NEEDED: 20 minutes, plus time for cooking the eggs.

✳ Cook's Notes: A foolproof method for cooking hard-boiled eggs is to cover the eggs with cool salted water. Then cover the pot and bring to a slow boil over medium heat. Once boiling, remove from the heat, leave covered, and allow water to cool to room temperature. Then, peel and use. With this method, no green or gray yolks.

Per Serving: Calories 170, Total fat 8g (Sat fat 2g/ Mono fat 4g/ Poly fat 2g) Cholesterol 187mg, Sodium 195mg, Carbs 13g, Fiber 2g, Protein 10g.

Territo Wedges With Guacamole

Call it Tex Mex, call it Southern comfort, call it whatever you want, but we guarantee you'll love it!

Makes 2 servings

1 medium-sized flour tortilla
(whole wheat preferred)
½ cup nonfat refried beans
¼ cup salsa
⅓ cup shredded light Monterey jack, cheddar, or
'Mexican' cheese mix
12 halved cherry tomatoes
⅓ cup shredded cooked chicken (optional)
2 tablespoons nonfat or low fat sour cream
Olive oil spray

Spray olive oil on nonstick skillet, and warm pan over low heat. Place tortilla on a large plate, and spread with a layer of refried beans. On one half of the tortilla, spread layers of salsa, cheese, tomato halves, and chicken if desired. Fold tortilla in half, and transfer to skillet. Heat until golden brown on one side, then turn tortilla over to brown other half. When golden brown and cheese is melted, transfer to plate and cut into 4 wedges. Top with dollops of sour cream, and serve immediately. These are good served with Guacamole (see recipe below). Also makes a good main course.

TIME NEEDED: 15 minutes

Per Serving: Calories 311, Total fat 9g (Sat fat 3g/ Mono fat 5g/ Poly fat 1g) Cholesterol 30mg, Sodium 448mg, Carbs 37g, Fiber 6g, Protein 21g.

Guacamole

Makes 2 servings

1 ripe avocado
½ small chopped tomato
1 thinly sliced green onion
Juice of ½ lemon
¼ teaspoon salt
1 tablespoon salsa

Mash avocado with fork in small bowl. Add remaining ingredients. Serve with Territo Wedges, steamed tortillas, or fat-free tortilla chips and extra salsa.

TIME NEEDED: 10 minutes

Per Serving: Calories 177, Total fat 16g (Sat fat 2g/ Mono fat 11g/ Poly fat 3g) Cholesterol 0mg, Sodium 316mg, Carbs 11g, Fiber 3g, Protein 3g.

A S K T H E
D O C T O R

"I thought avocados were off limits because they're so high in fat and calories. What's the deal?"

Just because avocados were blessed with quite a bit of fat doesn't mean they're not healthful. You've got to look beyond total fat content to the types of fats. Go easy on saturated fats, found primarily in meat and dairy products, because they increase the risk of heart disease. Partially hydrogenated oils, in margarine and most commercially baked and fried foods, should be avoided like the plague, for they contain trans fats, which are even more harmful than saturated fats.

The main type of fat in avocados is monounsaturated, and it actually benefits the cardiovascular system. Furthermore, avocados are a good source of a specialized fatty compound called beta-sitosterol, which helps lower cholesterol and protects against cancer.

88

South American Style Black Beans, Rice & Greens

This is also a great vegetarian main course.

Makes 8 servings

2 sliced onions

3 tablespoons lime juice

1 teaspoon hot sauce

1 cup low-sodium tomato juice

1½ cups low-sodium vegetable or chicken stock or broth

1 cup long-grain brown rice

2 chopped onions (divided use)

3 cloves minced garlic

1 chopped jalapeno pepper

1 can (28 oz) chunked plum tomatoes (with juice)

24 ounces cooked or canned black beans

2 cups chopped greens (one or more: kale, collards, spinach, bok choy, romaine, dandelion, etc.)

4 peeled oranges cut in small cubes

Water, as needed

Place sliced onions in a glass bowl and cover with boiling water. Let stand 5-10 minutes and drain. Add lime juice and hot sauce and cover for 30-45 minutes. At the same time, bring low-sodium tomato juice and broth to boil in a medium saucepan and stir in rice. Simmer until tender according to package directions. Meanwhile, in another saucepan, simmer one chopped onion, garlic, and jalapeno pepper in juice from canned tomatoes until onion is soft, about 8 minutes. Add half the beans and mash them with a fork into onion, garlic, and pepper. Add tomatoes and remaining beans and simmer for 30 minutes.

In a large stockpot, bring ½ cup water to boil, add remaining chopped onion and simmer about 5 minutes. Add greens and cook until tender and wilted. (Lettuce greens will only take a few minutes, but the others may need 15-20 minutes.) Drain. Serve bowls of rice topped with bean sauce. Let each person add greens, onions, and oranges as desired.

TIME NEEDED: A little less than 1 hour

Per Serving: Calories 293, Total fat 1g (Sat fat 0g/ Mono fat 0g/ Poly fat 1g) Cholesterol 0mg, Sodium 165mg, Carbs 59g, Fiber 12g, Protein 14g.

THE DOCTOR IS IN:

Virtually every culture in the world has its own version of beans and rice. No wonder: This low-cost combination provides high-quality protein with all the essential amino acids – something each lacks it itself.

Garlic Green Beans

These green beans have graduated from finishing school.

Makes 4 servings

1 large chopped onion

2 teaspoons olive oil

1 pound fresh or frozen green beans

6 cloves minced garlic or 1 tablespoon powdered garlic

1 teaspoon salt or salt substitute

In a large nonstick skillet, sauté onions in olive oil until onions become transparent. Add beans, garlic, and salt, and continue to cook, stirring often, for 2 minutes. Add ¼ cup water, cover, and steam until beans are tender. Just before serving, remove lid, turn up heat and boil off any excess liquid.

TIME NEEDED: 20 minutes

Per Serving: Calories 68, Total fat 2g (Sat fat 0g/ Mono fat 2g/ Poly fat 0g) Cholesterol 0mg, Sodium 541mg, Carbs11g, Fiber 4g, Protein 2g.

Layered Tostada With Homemade Salsa

Makes 4 servings

2 cups cooked pinto beans or 1 (16-ounce) can
fat-free refried beans
Salsa, homemade (see recipe on p. 149) or purchased
4 whole wheat tortillas
½ cup chopped red onion
1 cup shredded romaine lettuce
½ cup chopped green pepper
½ cup chopped tomatoes
½ cup grated cheddar cheese
¼ cup low-fat or nonfat sour cream

Puree pinto beans in food processor or blender with a little salsa (or use canned refried beans). Heat beans in a saucepan over medium heat for 3-4 minutes until hot. Heat a large non-stick skillet over high heat. Heat tortillas, one at a time, 1-2 minutes on each side. Spread ½ cup beans on each tortilla, and layer onions, lettuce, peppers, tomatoes, and cheese. Top with sour cream and salsa. May be eaten with a fork or rolled up burrito style.

TIME NEEDED: 20 minutes

Per Serving: Calories 438, Total fat 9g (Sat fat 4g/ Mono fat 4g/ Poly fat 1g) Cholesterol 16mg, Sodium 449mg, Carbs 68g, Fiber 11g, Protein 19g.

91

Portobello Pilaf

One can only wonder why bulgur, so delicious and popular in many parts of the world, has not become a staple in American homes. Slow-burning food that prepares quickly.

Makes 4 servings

1 ½ cups thinly sliced Portobello mushrooms
(or other mushrooms)
1 teaspoon olive oil
1 cup bulgur
2 cups low-sodium vegetable or chicken broth
2 green onions, thinly sliced
¼ teaspoon pepper

Sauté mushrooms in olive oil over medium heat in a medium saucepan, about five minutes. Add remaining ingredients, bring to a boil, then reduce heat, cover and simmer for 20 minutes or until all the liquid is absorbed. Fluff with a fork and serve.

TIME NEEDED: 30 minutes

✳ Cook's Notes: Brown rice, barley, oat groats (whole oats), quinoa, or other whole grains may be substituted for bulgur. Cooking time will vary: brown rice, barley, and oat groats will take 45-55 minutes, while quinoa will only take 15 minutes.

Per Serving: Calories 179, Total fat 2g (Sat fat 0g/ Mono fat 1g/ Poly fat 1g) Cholesterol 0mg, Sodium 31mg, Carbs 32g, Fiber 8g, Protein 12g.

fish main dishes

Have you ever made a New Year's resolution to eat more heart-healthy fish – and forgotten it even before the end of January? Why not systematically work your way through this section from beginning to end, trying just one or two recipes per week? Make a date with fish. Put it on your menu-planning calendar. This is one date that will never break your heart.

93

Newport Fish Tacos

A Southern California specialty.

Makes 4 hearty tacos

¼ cup nonfat sour cream

¼ cup nonfat mayonnaise

2 tablespoons chopped cilantro

1 teaspoon chili powder (divided use)

Olive oil spray

1 tablespoon lime juice

1 teaspoon extra-virgin olive oil

½ pound of fish fillets (cod, mahi-mahi, or halibut)

4 whole wheat tortillas

1 cup shredded cabbage

½ avocado, thinly sliced

4 lime wedges

¼ cup onion, thinly sliced

½ cup chopped tomato

Mix sour cream, mayonnaise, cilantro and ½ teaspoon chili powder in a small bowl and refrigerate. Combine lime juice, oil, and ½ teaspoon chili powder in a medium bowl. Preheat broiler and spray broiler pan with olive oil spray. Brush lime juice and oil mixture over fish. Place fish on broiler pan and cook 3-4 inches from heat for 5 minutes. Turn and broil 5 more minutes, until fish flakes easily with fork. Meanwhile, heat tortillas one at a time in a large nonstick skillet preheated over medium-high heat. Cook for about 30 seconds on each side, or until hot and pliable. Keep warm. Break fish into large flakes, and spoon into tortillas. Top with cabbage, avocado slices, and a scant tablespoon of sour cream sauce. Serve with lime wedges, onions and tomatoes.

TIME NEEDED: 30 minutes

✳ Cook's Notes: In coastal Orange County in Southern California where we live, fish taco stands are almost as common as hamburger joints. Try these. We think you'll like them.

Per Taco: Calories 404, Total fat 11g (Sat fat 2g/ Mono fat 7g/ Poly fat 2g) Cholesterol 26mg, Sodium 546mg, Carbs 48g, Fiber 4g, Protein 18g.

Lemon Pepper Salmon with Mixed Vegetables

Here's a one-pot wonder, but the pot is a steamer.

Makes 2 servings

2 tablespoons fresh lemon juice

1 tablespoon Dijon mustard

2 teaspoons olive oil

½ teaspoon coarsely ground black pepper

2 cloves minced garlic

2 cups water

2 medium leeks

4 fresh broccoli spears

2 cups sliced yellow squash

2 (4-ounce) salmon fillets, ½ inch thick

1 lemon cut into wedges

Combine lemon juice, mustard, oil, pepper, and garlic. Reserve 1 tablespoon mixture; spread remaining mixture on salmon and set aside. Remove outer leaves, tops and stems of leeks, leaving about 6 inches. Clean thoroughly. Cut in half lengthwise. Bring water to boil in the bottom of a steamer. Place leeks side by side in steamer over boiling water. Cover and steam for 4 minutes. Arrange broccoli across leeks, cover and steam for 2 minutes. Add squash slices over broccoli, then arrange salmon fillets on top. Cover and steam for 5 minutes until fish flakes easily with a fork. Serve fillets on top of vegetables, with a half-tablespoon dollop of mustard mixture on top of fillets.

Seafood Brochettes

As easy under the broiler as on the grill. Enjoy them year-round.

Makes 6 brochettes

½ cup dry sherry

2 tablespoons sesame oil

1 tablespoon crushed sesame seeds

1 minced clove garlic

¼ teaspoon salt

Freshly ground pepper to taste

2 tablespoons fresh grated ginger

6 medium peeled (except for tails)
and deveined shrimp

¾ pound sea scallops

½ pound fresh pineapple, cut into 1 inch wedges

12 cherry tomatoes

1 medium onion, cut into 6 wedges

1 large seeded green pepper, blanched 3 minutes
in boiling water and cut in 1 inch pieces

Combine sherry, sesame oil and seeds, garlic, salt, pepper, and ginger and pour over shrimp and scallops in a shallow glass or ceramic bowl. Cover and place in refrigerator for 30 minutes. Drain but reserve marinade. Pierce one shrimp on each skewer, along with scallops alternating with pineapple, tomatoes, onion and green pepper. Broil or grill the brochettes 4 - 6 inches from heat for 8 - 10 minutes, turning several times and brushing often with marinade, until seafood is cooked.

TIME NEEDED: 50 minutes

✳ Cook's Notes: You'll find wooden skewers in the cookware section of your grocery store or in specialty shops. Soaking them in water for at least 30 minutes before using helps to prevent them from charring when they're placed on the grill. If you make brochettes or shish-kebobs frequently, look for reusable metal skewers – they never break or char.

Per Brochette: Calories 161, Total fat 5g (Sat fat 1g/ Mono fat 2g/ Poly fat 2g) Cholesterol 34mg, Sodium 222mg, Carbs 9g, Fiber 1g, Protein 13g.

Mussels Cubane

Don't be daunted by shellfish. This recipe is deceptively simple.

Makes 4 servings

2 pounds clean fresh or frozen mussels in shell

Olive oil spray

2 medium onions, chopped

2 medium zucchini, sliced ¼ thick

1 medium eggplant, peeled and cubed

1 28-ounce can chopped low-sodium tomatoes (can use fresh)

1 (8 to 10-ounce) package frozen corn (can use fresh)

½ cup golden raisins

¼ teaspoon paprika

¼ teaspoon cayenne

Coat large nonstick skillet with olive oil spray. Sauté onions until transparent, about 5-7 minutes, over medium heat. Add zucchini, eggplant, tomatoes, corn, raisins, paprika and cayenne, and sauté another 5 minutes. Put vegetable mixture in stock pot, add mussels, bring to boil, lower. Lower heat and cover. Simmer about 10 minutes, shaking pot to toss contents occasionally, until most mussels have opened. Remove mussels with their shells (discard any unopened ones), and divide into four bowls. Pour vegetable mixture on top.

TIME NEEDED: 35 minutes

✳ Cook's Notes: Fresh mussels and clams tend to be seasonal, but frozen shellfish can be found year-round. When purchasing, look for tightly closed shells (or shells that close when you tap them) and a mild odor. Stored closely packed in the refrigerator, they'll remain fresh for a few days.

Per Serving: Calories 415, Total fat 5g (Sat fat 1g/ Mono fat 2g/ Poly fat 2g) Cholesterol 64mg, Sodium 682mg, Carbs 59g, Fiber 9g, Protein 34g.

poultry
main dishes

Instead of pondering the age-old query, "Which came first, the chicken or the egg?" consider a more practical question. Which of the two should come first on your shopping list? Both have a place on your table, but eggs should be eaten in moderation, while chicken should grace your table more frequently.

Ginger-Citrus Chicken

Citrus and poultry are a match made in heaven.

Makes 2 servings

2 lemons or limes
1 tablespoon low-sodium soy sauce
1-inch piece ginger root, minced
(or 2 teaspoons powdered ginger)
2 small or 1 large (halved) boneless,
skinless chicken breasts (½ pound total)

Juice the citrus and mix with soy sauce and ginger root. Place chicken breasts in a plastic bag. Add citrus and soy marinade, and rub into chicken. Close bag tightly and marinate for several hours or overnight. Preheat broiler, spray broiler pan with olive oil, and place chicken on broiler pan. Cook for 5-7 minutes on each side, depending on thickness.

TIME NEEDED: Preparation – 15 minutes; Marinating – several hours.

✳ Cook's Notes: Individually frozen boneless, skinless chicken breasts save a lot of time. Quickly defrost and use to create countless main-dish meals in minutes.

Per Serving: Calories 183, Total fat 7g (Sat fat 2g/ Mono fat 3g/ Poly fat 2g) Cholesterol 58mg, Sodium 359mg, Carbs 8g, Fiber 0g, Protein 20g.

Chicken Riviera

Piquant bits of green olive accentuate the vegetables' natural sweetness.

Makes 5 servings

½ teaspoon salt (divided use)
3 small boneless, skinless chicken breasts
(12 ounces total)
3 skinless chicken thighs
3 skinless chicken drumsticks
Olive oil spray
1½ chopped green bell peppers
½ cup chopped onion
18 green olives, pitted and sliced
1 clove minced garlic
2 medium thinly sliced zucchini
2 medium tomatoes peeled and cut into ¼-inch slices
¼ cup chopped parsley
1 tablespoon chopped fresh basil
(or 2 teaspoons dried basil)

Preheat oven to 375° F. Sprinkle ¼ teaspoon salt over chicken. Coat large nonstick skillet with olive oil spray. Add chicken, and cook over medium heat until browned on both sides (4-5 minutes per side). Remove from heat and place chicken in 13 x 9-inch baking dish (sprayed with olive oil). Put pepper, onion, olives, and garlic in skillet, and sauté over medium heat until garlic is slightly browned. Pour mixture over chicken, and follow with slices of zucchini, then slices of tomato. Sprinkle with remaining salt, parsley and basil. Cover baking dish, and cook for one hour.

TIME NEEDED: 1 hour, 15 minutes.

Per Serving: Calories 177, Total fat 6g (Sat fat 1g/ Mono fat 4g/ Poly fat 1g) Cholesterol 66mg, Sodium 432mg, Carbs 10g, Fiber 3g, Protein 23g.

THE DOCTOR IS IN:

Dark meat contains only slightly more fat than white breast meat. Remove the skin and you lose two-thirds to three-quarters of the fat, leaving dark meat with just 1 gram of saturated fat and a total fat content of 4 grams per 3 ounces of meat.

Chicken Marsala

See how the addition of one simple flavor – Marsala wine – can take chicken to unexpected heights.

Makes 4 servings

4 small or 2 large halved boneless, skinless chicken breasts (1 pound total)

¼ teaspoon pepper

¼ teaspoon salt

¼ cup flour

1 tablespoon olive oil

½ cup Marsala wine

½ cup low fat or nonfat chicken stock

½ lemon, juiced

1 cup sliced mushrooms

1 tablespoon chopped parsley

2 teaspoons flour (if needed)

Place chicken between two sheets of wax paper. Pound with a flat mallet until very thin (¼ inch). Mix pepper, salt, and flour together. Dredge chicken with seasoned flour to coat. (Shaking the chicken and seasoned flour in a plastic bag can accomplish this quickly.) Heat oil in a heavy skillet, and brown chicken on both sides over medium heat, about five minutes. Remove chicken and set aside. Add wine, stock, juice and mushrooms to skillet and stir. Reduce heat and cook until sauce is reduced, about ten minutes. (If sauce remains too thin, or you're impatient, add 2 teaspoons of flour to two tablespoons cold water, stir until dissolved, and stir into skillet). Return chicken breasts to skillet, coat with sauce, cover and simmer for 5-7 minutes or until chicken is warm and done. Garnish with parsley.

TIME NEEDED: 45 minutes

✳ Cook's Notes: Marsala, in western Sicily, has been exporting this unique wine for more than 200 years. Brandy was originally added to the wine to make it last during long ocean voyages. The taste stuck, and Marsala remains popular, particularly as a dessert and cooking wine. Make sure you use a real Italian Marsala – pale golden and semi-dry.

Per Serving: Calories 191, Total fat 7g (Sat fat 1g/ Mono fat 5g/ Poly fat 1g) Cholesterol 53mg, Sodium 260mg, Carbs 8g, Fiber 0g, Protein 24g.

Creamy Peppercorn Chicken

Green peppercorns are the same as the black variety but are harvested early before they become too hot. They impart tons of flavor without making the dish too spicy.

Makes 4 servings

4 small or 2 large halved boneless, skinless chicken breasts (1 pound total)
¼ teaspoon sea salt or seasoned salt
1 tablespoon crushed pink, green, or mixed peppercorns
Olive oil spray
½ cup dry sherry or orange juice
⅓ cup low-fat or nonfat sour cream
½ teaspoon tarragon or thyme leaves
2 teaspoons all purpose flour (if needed)

Place chicken between two sheets of wax paper. Pound breasts with flat mallet until very thin (¼ inch). Remove wax paper and sprinkle breasts with salt and crushed or coarsely ground peppercorns. Spray large nonstick skillet with olive oil. Add chicken and cook until done, about 5 minutes, over medium heat. Remove chicken and keep warm. Over high heat, add sherry or juice, and whisk in sour cream, tarragon or thyme. Boil until sauce is thickened and reduced by about half. (If sauce is too thin, add flour to two tablespoons cold water, mix until dissolved, and stir into skillet.) Spoon sauce over chicken.

TIME NEEDED: 20 minutes

✳ Cook's Notes: The word sherry comes from Jerez, the area in Andalusia in Southern Spain where this wine originated. Selecting the right sherry can be challenging, for these wines range from dry to sweet. For this dish select a nice dry sherry – and never use cooking sherry. It is usually just a low-quality sherry with added salt.

Per Serving: Calories 169, Total fat 5g (Sat fat 0g/ Mono fat 4g/ Poly fat 0g) Cholesterol 55mg, Sodium 208mg, Carbs 5g, Fiber 0g, Protein 23g.

vegetarian main dishes

It's no secret that vegetarians can revise recipes by simply omitting the meat called for, or that meat-lovers will just as often add meat to vegetarian recipes. However, we've developed vegetarian masterpieces that sport a rich balance of seasonings and wholesomeness. We think you'll enjoy the depth of flavor, satisfying textures and color combinations.

Buddha's Feast With Buckwheat Noodles

Find out why the popularity of these soba noodles is moving across the nation at jet speed.

Makes 5 servings

10 ounces buckwheat noodles (soba or
other noodles such as linguine)

3 cups low-sodium vegetable or
chicken stock (divided use)

2 tablespoons low-sodium soy sauce

2 tablespoons apple juice or brown rice syrup

½ teaspoon grated ginger

½ teaspoon dried red pepper flakes
(to taste – these are hot)

1 clove minced garlic

2 tablespoons cornstarch

1½ teaspoons sesame oil

1 large carrot, diagonally sliced

2 cups bite-sized broccoli florets

1 medium zucchini, diagonally sliced

1 red or green pepper, cut into 1-inch cubes

½ pound snow peas

1 cup sliced mushrooms

2 cups coarsely chopped bok choy or
Napa cabbage

Bring a large pan of water to a boil and cook noodles as directed until just tender (al dente). Set aside and keep warm. Meanwhile, in a small sauce pan, mix 2 cups of the stock, soy sauce, apple juice, ginger, pepper flakes, garlic, and cornstarch, and bring to a boil. Stir until thickened, then remove from heat, add oil and keep warm. In another large pan or steamer, steam vegetables in the remaining cup of broth, starting with carrots and broccoli, then adding remaining vegetables after 2 minutes. Steam for another 2-3 minutes until vegetables are tender, yet firm. Mix together in a large serving bowl with the cooked, drained and rinsed noodles, vegetables, and sauce, stirring well to cover with sauce.

TIME NEEDED: 35 minutes

❈ Cook's Notes: Soba (buckwheat noodles) are a favorite in Japan, where they are eaten cold, dipped in soy sauce with green onions and grated horse-radish, or hot in peppery soups. Rinse them well after cooking, for they tend to stick together.

Per Serving: Calories 325, Total fat 2g (Sat fat 0g/ Mono fat 1g/ Poly fat 1g) Cholesterol 0mg, Sodium 591mg, Carbs 58g, Fiber 5g, Protein 18g.

Joe's Special

Though the origins of Joe's Special are clouded in the mists of history, some say it was created at a San Francisco restaurant as an after-hours snack for dance-band musicians in the 1920s. Although the original called for ground beef, we think you'll like this healthier vegetarian version.

Makes 4 servings

½ pound trimmed fresh spinach (or a 10-ounce package of frozen spinach)
Olive oil spray
1 small finely diced onion
½ pound sliced mushrooms
2 eggs
⅛ teaspoon pepper
⅛ teaspoon dried dill

Steam spinach, drain off any water and set aside. Spray a large nonstick skillet with olive oil and sauté onions for about five minutes over low heat. Add mushrooms and sauté five minutes more. Combine eggs, spinach, pepper and dill, and mix well. Pour egg mixture over mushrooms and onions and cook over medium heat, stirring constantly until eggs are set but not dry. Serve immediately.

TIME NEEDED: 20 minutes

Per Serving: Calories 69, Total fat 3g (Sat fat 1g/ Mono fat 1g/ Poly fat 1g) Cholesterol 94mg, Sodium 76mg, Carbs 7g, Fiber 3g, Protein 6g.

California Pasta Primavera

Broccoli for cancer protection, garlic to bolster your immune system, and all this garden freshness to rejuvenate your soul.

Makes 6 servings

8 ounces linguine
Olive oil spray
2 cloves minced garlic
1 pound bite-sized broccoli florets
1 pound thinly sliced zucchini
1 pound thinly sliced fresh mushrooms
8 ounces ripe chopped tomatoes
1 tablespoon olive oil
1 to 2 tablespoons water
2 tablespoons grated Parmesan cheese

Cook linguine according to package directions, and when done, drain and return to pot. While the pasta is cooking, steam florets until just tender (al dente), and set aside. Spray a large nonstick skillet with olive oil, heat over medium heat, add garlic, zucchini and mushrooms and cook for 5 minutes. Add broccoli and tomatoes. Mix well and cook 2 minutes more. Stir in olive oil and water. Add the vegetable mixture and Parmesan to the pasta and toss to combine.

TIME NEEDED: 30 minutes

✳ Cook's Notes: The Parmesan cheese most Americans are familiar with (grated, in shakers, and unrefrigerated) is a pale imitation of "real" Parmesan cheese: Italy's Parmigiano-Reggiano. Made from skimmed or partially skimmed milk and aged at least two years, this magnificent hard cheese releases a burst of flavor when you grate it just before using.

Per Serving: Calories 214, Total fat 3g (Sat fat 1g/ Mono fat 1g/ Poly fat 1g) Cholesterol 1mg, Sodium 62mg, Carbs 40g, Fiber 5g, Protein 10g.

Idel's Asparagus And Leek Tart

To make this dish go together in a snap, precook the asparagus using the microwave method: Place in a microwave-safe dish, add 3 tablespoons water, cover, and cook for 3 to 5 minutes.

Makes 6 servings

½ cup whole-wheat bread crumbs

1 to 2 teaspoons olive oil

½ pound asparagus, trimmed and cut into 2 inch pieces

1 tablespoon olive oil

2 leeks sliced (white part only)

2 tablespoons flour

1 cup frozen egg whites or 8 egg whites, lightly beaten

1 cup fat free ricotta cheese

¼ cup shredded low fat, low sodium Swiss cheese

½ cup skim milk

¼ teaspoon nutmeg

Preheat oven to 425° F. Mix bread crumbs with 1-2 teaspoons olive oil and pat onto bottom and sides of a pie pan. Bake in oven for 5-6 minutes or until browned. Meanwhile, bring 2 cups water to boil in a large saucepan. Plunge asparagus into water, blanch for 2 to 3 minutes, drain, and set aside. (Or use the microwave as described above.) In a medium non-stick skillet, heat olive oil and leeks over medium heat and cook for 4 to 5 minutes. Sprinkle flour over leeks, stir to coat, and transfer mixture to a large bowl. Add asparagus, eggs, ricotta and Swiss cheese, milk, and nutmeg, and mix again. Pour mixture into pie pan over bread crumbs. Bake until puffy and brown, about 40 minutes. Let stand 10 minutes before slicing.

TIME NEEDED: 50 minutes

❇ Cook's Notes: Substituting the usual piecrust with a thin "crust" of whole wheat breadcrumbs in this recipe reaps big savings in calories and saturated fat. Try this "crustless" approach with quiches and pies as well.

Per Serving: Calories 169, Total fat 4g (Sat fat 1g/ Mono fat 3g/ Poly fat 0g) Cholesterol 9mg, Sodium 260mg, Carbs 17g, Fiber 1g, Protein 15g.

desserts &
beverages

Here are a few recipes to satisfy your sweet tooth – without having to worry about your blood sugar or your waistline. Most of these recipes contain fruit, so they provide a healthy array of fiber, antioxidants and other nutrients along with good taste.

Fresh Fruit Parfait

Is it any wonder that fruit has been a favorite subject of artists through the ages?

Makes 2 servings

1 cup plain nonfat yogurt

2 teaspoons xylitol, or 1 to 2 drops of stevia

½ teaspoon vanilla extract

½ sliced banana

½ cup sliced strawberries

1 sliced, peeled kiwi fruit

½ cup Mandarin oranges, drained

Add sweetener and vanilla to yogurt and stir well. In two parfait or wine glasses (or bowls), layer fruit, then yogurt, then fruit and so on. Variations: Which fruits are in season? Which fruits do you have on hand?

TIME NEEDED: 10 minutes

Per Serving: Calories 151, Total fat 1g (Sat fat 1g/ Mono fat 0g/ Poly fat 0g) Cholesterol 2mg, Sodium 90mg, Carbs 30g, Fiber 4g, Protein 8g.

ASK THE DOCTOR

"What fruits and vegetables are best for my five servings each day?"

The US Department of Agriculture measures a food's oxygen radical absorbance capacity (ORAC) to define which foods have greater antioxidant activity. (See p.185 for more useful antioxidant information.) According to USDA ranking, in descending order, the top 10 ORAC fruits are prunes, raisins, blueberries, blackberries, strawberries, raspberries, plums, oranges, red grapes, and cherries. The ten highest ORAC vegetables are garlic, kale, spinach, Brussels sprouts, alfalfa sprouts, broccoli florets, beets, red bell peppers, onions, and corn.

Peach Cobbler

A great way to end lunch, but you might find yourself boxing some up for an afternoon snack.

Makes 6 servings

1 cup pineapple juice

1 teaspoon vanilla

1 teaspoon cinnamon

1 tablespoon tapioca powder

Olive oil pan spray

2 ½ cups sliced peaches (frozen also good)

⅓ cup chopped almonds

⅓ cup oatmeal

Preheat oven to 350° F. Blend juice, vanilla, cinnamon, and tapioca. Spray a pie pan with olive oil, then spread the peaches in the pan. Pour the juice mixture over the fruit. Combine almonds and oatmeal and sprinkle evenly over the fruit. Bake for 45 minutes.

✳ Cook's Notes: The window for purchasing decent fresh peaches is maddeningly short. The good news is that frozen peaches are surprisingly tasty – and hands down better than canned peaches.

Per Serving: Calories 133, Total fat 5g (Sat fat 1g/ Mono fat 3g/ Poly fat 1g) Cholesterol 0mg, Sodium 1mg, Carbs 20g, Fiber 2g, Protein 3g.

Oatmeal Cookies

The needed indulgence. No sugar and cardiovascular-friendly oatmeal and walnuts are the redeeming features.

Makes 4 - 5 dozen cookies
⅓ cup butter (organic preferred)
or organic solid coconut oil
2 eggs
½ cup xylitol
1 teaspoon vanilla
1 cup whole wheat flour
¼ teaspoon baking soda
¼ teaspoon salt
½ teaspoon cinnamon
2 cups slow-cooking oatmeal
1 cup chopped walnuts

In a large mixing bowl, beat butter or coconut oil, eggs, xylitol and vanilla. Mix soda, salt, cinnamon and flour, then add to wet ingredients, along with nuts, and mix well. Drop onto nonstick cookie sheet lightly sprayed with olive oil pan spray. Bake at 350° F. approximately 10 minutes.

TIME NEEDED: 50 minutes

Per Cookie: Calories 52, Total fat 3g (Sat fat 1g/ Mono fat 1g/Poly fat 1g) Cholesterol 11mg, Sodium 33mg, Carbs 4g, Fiber 1g, Protein 2g.

116

Ginger Lemonade

An unequaled drink when you have a cold or the flu. You get the liquid you need, plus the vitamin C and the anti-inflammatory power of ginger. Also an elegant addition to a meal in place of plain water.

Makes 3 to 4 glasses
1½ tablespoons fresh lemon juice
½ teaspoon freshly grated ginger juice
25-ounce bottle of sparkling mineral water
2 to 4 drops stevia liquid, or to taste

Juice half a lemon and strain out seeds. Measure 1½ tablespoons into a pitcher. Grate a 2-inch chunk of peeled ginger and press out the juice through a fine strainer. Add the ½ teaspoon of ginger juice to the pitcher, along with the mineral water and stevia. Stir well. Pour over ice if desired. Note: This isn't rocket science; more or less of the lemon, ginger, and sweetener can be added to taste.

Per Serving: Calories 2, Total fat 0g (Sat fat 0g/ Mono fat 0g/ Poly fat 0g) Cholesterol 0mg, Sodium 2mg, Carbs 1g, Fiber 1g, Protein 0g.

THE DOCTOR IS IN:

Ginger remains a pungent favorite in Asian and Indian cuisine, but it also has a long history of medicinal benefits. Its ability to curtail inflammation is currently a hot research topic, but its oldest use is to quell nausea. It is more effective than Dramamine for preventing motion sickness and helps with morning sickness during pregnancy and postsurgical nausea.

Evening Meals

Dinner time at home provides the perfect haven for leisurely dining. Among these recipes for evening meals, you can expect to find everything from comfort foods (Connie's Chicken Soup) to remodeled traditional (Steve's Buffalo Chili) to sustainable chic (Chicken-Lime Chopped Salad).

dinners that revitalize

As you relax through the evening hours, your body does not have the calorie demands that it does when you are going full-steam during the day. These dinners have been specially formulated to give you the lightness that will serve you well at the end of the day. If you prepare desserts, dish up modest portions that are just big enough to satisfy without taxing your digestive system. Also, eating several hours before retiring will improve digestion and facilitate sleep.

soups & stews

When making soup, think washtub! Make it in volume — double or triple the recipe if it only makes a few servings. Then enjoy the leftovers or freeze individual-sized servings for quick meals later on. Most soups end up with a lot of sodium, because canned stock and bouillon cubes are loaded with the stuff. When buying stock or broth, look for the nonfat, low-sodium varieties that are now available.

Connie's Chicken Soup

For whatever ails you...or to make sure that nothing will.

Makes 8 servings

1 whole chicken, or 3-4 pounds
chicken bones and parts
1 onion, diced
2 cloves garlic, sliced
1 bay leaf
2 carrots, sliced
3 stalks celery, sliced
1 teaspoon salt or salt substitute
½ teaspoon black pepper
1 pound package of egg noodles

Wash chicken and combine it with all ingredients except for the noodles in a large stock pot. Cover completely with water, bring to a boil, and skim off and discard the first gray foam that forms. Then reduce heat to a simmer and cook for at least 1 hour, preferably 2 hours, until chicken is very tender. Near the end of the cooking time, in a separate pot cook the noodles as directed until just tender (al dente). Remove the chicken from the soup, cool and discard the skin and bones. Skim the fat off the soup. Cut the chicken into bite-sized pieces and return to the pot. Add more water to achieve desired concentration, adjust the seasonings, and add the cooked noodles. Heat to serving temperature.

TIME NEEDED: 10 minutes preparation, 1 to 2 hours for cooking.

Per Serving: Calories 373; Total fat 3g (Sat fat 1g/ Mono fat 1g/ Poly fat 1g) Cholesterol 90mg, Sodium 133mg, Carbs 44g, Fiber 3g, Protein 32g.

THE DOCTOR IS IN:

Whenever anyone in our house gets sick, my wife Connie cooks up a big pot of chicken soup. According to a 2000 study, chicken soup improves hydration and nutritional status and relieves congestion by increasing the flow of mucus. In addition, it inhibits the inflammatory response that causes many of the symptoms of colds and flu.

Steve's Buffalo Chili

Chili that can stand up to the best – with an unusual twist.

Makes 8 servings

1 pound ground buffalo

1 large onion, chopped

¾ cup boiling water

20 ounces chopped canned tomatoes with juice
(Mexican or Chili spiced is good)

20 ounces canned red kidney beans with juice

⅛ teaspoon paprika

1 to 2 tablespoons chili powder

Olive oil spray

8 tablespoons low-fat or non-fat sour cream

8 tablespoons low-fat or 'light' shredded cheddar

Spray stockpot with olive oil. Sauté buffalo meat until brown. Add all other ingredients except sour cream and cheddar. Bring to boil, then reduce heat to simmer, stirring occasionally for at least one hour (flavor will continue to develop with extra cooking time). Garnish each serving with a tablespoon of sour cream and cheddar. (Note: May be served over rice.)

TIME NEEDED: 1 to 2 hours of cooking time, 10 minutes preparation

✳ Cook's Notes: Buffalo meat (technically called bison) contains just one-quarter of the fat of trimmed beef. Furthermore, the small but growing number of bison ranchers grass feed their animals and do not give them growth hormones or antibiotics. You'll find it in larger grocery and health food stores, or it may be special ordered.

Per Serving: Calories 417; Total fat 10g (Sat fat 4g/ Mono fat 5g/ Poly fat 1g) Cholesterol 42mg, Sodium 205mg, Carbs 49g, Fiber 12g, Protein 30g.

Lazy "Beef" Stew

Where's the beef? It's in the stock! This is a crockpot stew, so it sets the cook free.

Makes 6 servings

1 pound ground turkey breast

3 cups low-sodium beef stock

10 small new red potatoes, cut in half

1 pound baby carrots or regular carrots cut into 1-inch slices

2 peeled, quartered onions

3 stalks of trimmed celery cut into 1-inch slices

15-ounces low-sodium canned stewed tomatoes (Italian style preferred)

3 bay leaves

1½ tablespoons Worchester sauce

¼ teaspoon curry powder

¼ teaspoon poultry seasoning

⅛ teaspoon cayenne

½ teaspoon salt or salt substitute

½ teaspoon black pepper

In a large nonstick skillet over medium high heat, cook turkey until almost cooked through, about 5 minutes. Place all ingredients in a large crockpot, stir well, cover, and cook on low heat for 6 hours.

TIME NEEDED: From 2 to 6 hours, depending on the method.

 Cook's Notes: If you don't have a crockpot, simmer this stew over very low heat for about two hours. Stir occasionally and add more stock if it gets too thick.

Per Serving: Calories 250; Total fat 1g (Sat fat 1g/ Mono fat 0g/ Poly fat 0g) Cholesterol 50mg, Sodium 329mg, Carbs 34g, Fiber 5g, Protein 28g.

Indian Mulligatawny Soup

With or without meat, there is no faster soup with so much flavor. You can worry about learning how to pronounce it later.

Makes 4 servings

1 tablespoon olive oil

½ cup chopped onion

½ cup chopped carrot

½ cup chopped celery

½ cup green pepper

½ cup chopped apple

Dash crushed red pepper

¾ teaspoon curry powder

3 cups low-sodium chicken or vegetarian stock

¾ cup pureed garbanzo beans

1 tablespoon arrowroot or cornstarch, mixed with

¼ cup water

1 cup shredded cooked chicken

Parsley (for garnish)

Sauté vegetables, apple, red pepper and curry powder in olive oil over low to medium heat until tender, about 10 minutes. Heat stock in a saucepan to boiling point. Pureé the garbanzo beans in a food processor or blender, adding water as needed. Add the bean mixture to the boiling stock and bring back to a boil. Add sautéed vegetables, chicken (optional) and arrowroot or cornstarch mixture. Cook, stirring often, until hot and thick, about 3-5 minutes. Garnish with chopped parsley.

TIME NEEDED: 25 minutes

✳ Cook's Notes: This soup originated in colonial India. Mulligatawny means "pepper water."

Per Serving: Calories 192; Total fat 5g (Sat fat 1g/ Mono fat 3g/ Poly fat 1g) Cholesterol 30mg, Sodium 437mg, Carbs 19g, Fiber 3g, Protein 23g.

salads

Eat salads often. Raw vegetables contain a cornucopia of essential nutrients – and the deeper the color, the more nutritious. Move away from iceberg lettuce and experiment with new types of salad greens. For added fiber and nutrition, toss in additional raw veggies, cooked beans, or freshly ground flaxseed. Most any salad can be turned into a spectacular main dish by topping it with a seasoned grilled, broiled, or sautéed breast of chicken or fillet of fish.

High-Protein Fruit Salad

Couple this healthy salad with a bowl of soup for a light, satisfying supper.

Makes 2 servings

½ apple cut into chunks

½ pear cut into chunks

½ cup blueberries, strawberries, or blackberries

½ cup cubed cantaloupe, honeydew or other melon

2 tablespoons raw sunflower seeds

2 tablespoons raw almonds

2 tablespoons raw pumpkin seeds

1 cup plain, non-fat yogurt

1 tablespoon sugar-free jam (your choice of flavor)

Mix fruit, seeds and nuts. Stir jam into yogurt and pour over fruit-nut mixture.

TIME NEEDED: 10 minutes

Per Serving: Calories 285; Total fat 9g (Sat fat 1g/ Mono fat 4g/ Poly fat 4g) Cholesterol 2mg, Sodium 96mg, Carbs 39g, Fiber 6g, Protein 12g.

THE DOCTOR IS IN:

Raw nuts and seeds are a concentrated source of high-quality protein and healthful fats. At the Whitaker Wellness Institute, we recommend that our diabetic patients snack on a small handful (about 2 tablespoons) of mixed raw nuts and seeds between meals. This high-protein, low-carb snack helps keep blood sugar levels in check.

Southwestern Salad

Equally as wonderful made with cubed, leftover chicken or turkey.

Makes 2 servings

½ pound ground turkey or chicken breast
Olive oil pan spray
1 teaspoon chili powder
¼ teaspoon salt
⅛ teaspoon black pepper
3 cups lettuce (Romaine preferred) torn into bite-sized pieces
¼ cup thinly sliced onion
1 coarsely chopped tomato
½ coarsely chopped avocado
¼ cup sliced black olives
½ cup corn, preferably fresh; canned or frozen acceptable
4 tablespoons grated low-fat cheddar, pepper-jack or Asiago cheese

Brown ground turkey or chicken in medium nonstick skillet with olive oil spray over medium-high heat, adding chili powder, salt and pepper. Drain and set aside. Combine remaining ingredients in large bowl, add chicken or turkey and mix well. Top with seasoned meat. Serve with Chili Ranch Dressing. (See recipe below.)

TIME NEEDED: (For salad and dressing) 25minutes

Cook's Notes: Half of this salad's appeal is in the contrasting colors. To realize the avocado's vibrant green, don't cut it up until you are just ready to mix and serve.

Per Serving (salad and dressing): Calories 405; Total fat 17g (Sat fat 4g/ Mono fat 10g/ Poly fat 3g) Cholesterol 79mg, Sodium 854mg, Carbs 28g, Fiber 5g, Protein 34g.

Chili Ranch Dressing

Bottled salad dressing makes this a snap to prepare.

Makes 2 servings

4 tablespoons fat-free or low-fat ranch dressing
½ teaspoon chili powder

Mix chili powder into ranch dressing. Serve with Southwestern Salad.

134

Shanghai Chicken Salad

If you cook the chicken ahead of time, this salad will take 20 minutes – no time at all, compared with a round-trip to China.

Makes 2 servings

1 large chicken breast, cooked, thinly sliced and chilled

2 cups butter lettuce or spring mix

2 cups fresh chopped spinach

2 green onions, chopped

1 cup fresh bean sprouts

2 tablespoons toasted sesame seeds

After cooking, chicken can be flash-chilled in the freezer. Combine chicken with Sesame-Soy Dressing (recipe below). Let sit for ten minutes. Mix salad ingredients in serving bowl. Add chicken-dressing mixture. Toss with sesame seeds and serve.

TIME NEEDED: (For salad and dressing) 40 minutes

✳ Cook's Notes: Mung bean sprouts, the kind used in Asian cooking, should be purchased no more than a day or two before using, because they won't last much longer than that in the refrigerator. If you need to store them longer, place them in a jar, cover with water, and refrigerate. This should extend their freshness to a week. Rinse well before using.

Per Serving (salad and dressing): Calories 357; Total fat 19g (Sat fat 3g/ Mono fat 8g/ Poly fat 8g) Cholesterol 72mg, Sodium 396mg, Carbs 11g, Fiber 4g, Protein 32g.

135

Sesame-Soy Dressing

The tartness of lemon is a perfect match for soy sauce.

Makes 2 servings

2 tablespoons sesame oil

1 tablespoon low-sodium soy sauce

2 tablespoons lemon juice

1 small clove garlic, minced

½ teaspoon grated lemon peel

Mix all ingredients in a small bowl and stir. Serve with Shanghai Chicken Salad.

Chicken-Lime Chopped Salad

Got leftover chicken? Other lean meats also substitute well. In just 15 minutes you can have this main-course salad that is brimming with flavor, fiber, and a touch of class.

Makes 2 servings

2 cups chopped Romaine lettuce
2 medium chopped tomatoes
1 chopped ripe avocado
2 chopped celery stalks
2 chopped radishes
1 chopped medium or small cucumber
1 cup chopped cooked chicken breast, chilled

Combine vegetables in salad bowl. Mix chicken with lime vinaigrette (see recipe below). Toss chicken-vinaigrette mixture with vegetables and serve.

TIME NEEDED: (For salad and dressing) 20 minutes

Cook's Notes: You can substitute other types of lettuce for Romaine – but don't use iceberg lettuce. Although iceberg is America's favorite, it is the least nutritional member of the lettuce family. Romaine has six times more vitamin C than iceberg and up to ten times more beta-carotene. Greens like arugula, chicory, spinach, and radicchio are even more nutritious.

Per Serving (salad and vinaigrette): Calories 477; Total fat 28g (Sat fat 6g/ Mono fat 18g/ Poly fat 4g) Cholesterol 80mg, Sodium 399mg, Carbs 22g, Fiber 7g, Protein 34g.

Lime Vinaigrette

Makes 2 servings

2 tablespoons freshly squeezed lime juice
1 tablespoon extra virgin olive oil
1 fresh small garlic clove, minced
Salt and pepper to taste
xylitol or stevia (optional)

Blend ingredients together. Add a bit of xylitol or stevia to mellow the tartness if desired. Serve with Chicken-Lime Chopped Salad.

Roasted Vegetables With Mustard Vinaigrette

You're going to be asked to fix these again.

Makes 4 servings
1 eggplant, thinly sliced
2 small zucchini, sliced
½ pound sliced raw mushrooms or whole
Portobello mushrooms
1 to 2 tablespoons olive oil

Preheat broiler. Place vegetables on broiling pan and brush lightly with olive oil. Roast under broiler three or four minutes on each side. Let cool. Place vegetables on individual salad plates. Top with a spoonful of Mustard Vinaigrette. (Recipe below).

TIME NEEDED: (For vegetables and dressing) 20 minutes

❋ Cook's Notes: Vegetables can also be grilled on the barbecue over medium heat. Brush olive oil on both sides before placing them on the grill. Cooking time will depend on thickness but shouldn't be more than two or three minutes per side. Watch them carefully and turn only once.

Per Serving (vegetables and vinaigrette): Calories 166; Total fat 12g (Sat fat 2g/ Mono fat 9g/ Poly fat 1g) Cholesterol 0mg, Sodium 142mg, Carbs 14g, Fiber 5g, Protein 4g.

139

Mustard Vinaigrette

3 tablespoons vinegar
2 tablespoons olive oil
½ teaspoon mustard powder
¼ teaspoon celery seed
Pinch of black pepper
¼ teaspoon seasoned salt
(or salt substitute) to taste
1 clove garlic, minced

Mix all ingredients well. Serve with Roasted Vegetables. (See recipe above.)

appetizers & snacks

Sometimes an appetizer can substitute nicely for the conventional salad. The recipes that we offer here take just minutes of preparation, plus some cooking or chilling time. Now ain't that appetizin'!

Vegetable Kabobs

Pre-steaming the broccoli for just 3 minutes gives optimal color and texture.

Makes 4 servings

1 celery stalk cut in 1" pieces
1 package cherry tomatoes
1 small zucchini cut in 1" pieces
1 small head broccoli cut into florets
1 medium red or green bell pepper cut in 1" cubes
8 (6") bamboo skewers

On each bamboo skewer, spear one piece of celery, tomato, zucchini, broccoli and pepper. Serve with Creamy Artichoke Dip.

TIME NEEDED: (For vegetables and dip) 15 minutes

✳ Cook's Notes: Sure, you could just arrange these vegetables on a plate, but the skewers raise them up a notch or two.

Per Serving (kabobs and dip): Calories 139; Total fat 1g (Sat fat 1g/ Mono fat 0g/ Poly fat 0g) Cholesterol 3mg, Sodium 331mg, Carbs 22g, Fiber 9g, Protein 15g.

Creamy Artichoke Dip

Makes about 2 cups

1 cup canned water-packed artichokes, drained
½ teaspoon onion powder
1 cup fat-free or low-fat cottage cheese
2 to 3 tablespoons fat-free milk
2 diced green onions

Place all ingredients in blender or food processor and blend until smooth. Chill well before serving. (May substitute nonfat or low-fat sour cream for cottage cheese and milk.)

143

Roasted Garlic Spread

Left-over roasted garlic can be refrigerated and served again within a couple of days, or it makes a wonderful addition to pastas, soups, sauces or gravies.

Makes 4 servings
2 heads of garlic
2 teaspoons olive oil

Preheat oven to 325° F. Cut about 1/4 inch off the top of the garlic heads, leaving the tops of the cloves exposed. Place on a large piece of heavy-duty aluminum foil. Drizzle olive oil over garlic. Seal tightly and bake for 35-40 minutes. To serve, place on a plate with some whole-grain crackers or bread. To eat, remove individual cloves, squeeze out garlic (it will be soft), and spread on bread or crackers. Roasted garlic is delicious – and very, very mild, compared to fresh garlic.

TIME NEEDED: 5 minutes preparation, plus baking time.

✳ Cook's Notes: Don't be put off by the whole heads of garlic this recipe calls for. Roasting dramatically mellows out the flavor of garlic, and the result is delightful.

Per Serving: Calories 22; Total fat 2g (Sat fat 0g/ Mono fat 2g/ Poly fat 0g) Cholesterol 0mg, Sodium 0mg, Carbs 1g, Fiber 1g, Protein 0g.

Mushroom Pâté

Finely chopping the onions and mushrooms with a food processor cuts preparation time by almost 10 minutes.

Makes enough for 8
2 finely diced onions
3 cloves minced garlic
1 tablespoon olive oil
5 cups finely diced mushrooms
½ cup dry white wine (or low-sodium chicken or vegetable stock)
Pinch of thyme
½ teaspoon salt
1½ tablespoons arrowroot or cornstarch
3 tablespoons stock
Black or red pepper (optional)

Sauté the onions and garlic in olive oil until some golden color is noted. Add the mushrooms, wine or stock, thyme, and salt. Cook covered about 5 minutes until vegetables are soft. Mix arrowroot or cornstarch in 3 tablespoons stock, pour into skillet, and continue to cook, stirring constantly until thickened. Spoon into serving bowl and serve warm or chill until cold. Serve with whole-grain crackers. Variation: After chilling the mixture, add 2 tablespoons nonfat sour cream.

TIME NEEDED: 30 minutes preparation, plus time for chilling.

Per Serving: Calories 50; Total fat 1g (Sat fat 0g/ Mono fat 1g/ Poly fat 0g) Cholesterol 0mg, Sodium 185mg, Carbs 7g, Fiber 1g, Protein 2g. Roasted Garlic Spread

fish main dishes

Cold-water fish are among the most healthful of all foods because of their omega-3 fatty acids. Try to eat a serving or two a week of salmon, trout, tuna, sardines, or mackerel. Fish is easy to prepare – broiling, grilling, and sautéing only take a few minutes, and baking just a little longer. Although you can spruce fish up with marinades and sauces, all it really requires is a little lemon, olive oil, salt, and pepper.

Festival Sea Bass

This deliciously simple preparation, which works equally well with mahi-mahi, sole, or other favorites, will help to expand your fish repertoire.

Makes 4 servings

1 tablespoon olive oil
1 tablespoon fresh lime juice
1 tablespoon chopped fresh cilantro
Olive oil spray
4 sea bass fillets (5 ounces each)
Salt and pepper

Combine the olive oil, lime juice, and cilantro. Spray a baking sheet with additional olive oil, and place fillets on it. Brush fillets with oil mixture, sprinkle with salt and pepper. Time permitting, cover with plastic wrap and refrigerate for 20 minutes. Preheat oven to 425° F. Remove plastic wrap from fillets and bake for 15 minutes or until just cooked. Top fillets with salsa (see recipe below) and serve.

TIME NEEDED: (for fish and salsa): 25 minutes for preparation, 35 for marinating and baking.

Per Serving (fish and salsa): Calories 256; Total fat 13g (Sat fat 2g/ Mono fat 9g/ Poly fat 2g)Cholesterol 58mg, Sodium 371mg, Carbs 4g, Fiber 1g, Protein 27g.

Salsa

Use this homemade salsa with any Mexican dish.

Makes 4 servings

2 large ripe tomatoes
2 tablespoons chopped scallions
2 tablespoons chopped fresh cilantro
2 teaspoons minced garlic
2 tablespoons olive oil
½ tablespoon fresh lime juice
1-2 fresh or canned jalepeño peppers
(optional, to taste)
Salt and pepper to taste

Combine tomatoes, scallions, cilantro, garlic, olive oil, lime juice and jalepeños if desired. Add salt and pepper to taste.

Herbed Salmon With Papaya-Mango Chili Salsa

You're about to find out why first-class restaurants command top prices for entrées of fish and tropical fruit.

Makes 4 servings

2 tablespoons Dijon mustard

2 tablespoons fresh lemon juice

1 tablespoon chopped fresh thyme
(or 1 teaspoon dried thyme)

½ teaspoon ground pepper

4 salmon steaks (4 ounce, 1 inch thick)

1½ tablespoons canned minced mild green chilies

1 cup diced fresh papaya

1 cup diced fresh mango

2 tablespoons finely chopped red onion

Combine mustard, lemon juice, thyme, and pepper. Place salmon on glass or ceramic dish and cover with marinade. Cover and refrigerate for 2-3 hours, turning every hour. Combine chilies, papaya, mango, and onion in small dish and set aside.

When marinating is finished, preheat broiler. Lay salmon steaks on broiler pan and cook 4 minutes per side or until fork tender. Spoon salsa over salmon steaks and serve.

TIME NEEDED: 15-minute preparation, about 2 hours for marinating and broiling.

Per Serving: Calories 182; Total fat 4g (Sat fat 1g/ Mono fat 1g/ Poly fat 2g) Cholesterol 59mg, Sodium 172mg, Carbs 12g, Fiber 2g, Protein 23g.

THE DOCTOR IS IN:

Select wild salmon over farmed. Farmed isn't necessarily bad, but you should know that these fish come by their pink color and omega-3 fats not by eating krill and algae but from pigments and oils added to their feed. The best salmon of all, and the least endangered, is wild Alaska salmon.

Lemon Mustard Grilled Halibut With Tarragon

A perfect way to introduce yourself to cooking with tarragon.

Makes 4 servings
½ cup fresh lemon juice

1 tablespoon minced lemon zest

¼ cup Dijon mustard

3 tablespoons finely chopped tarragon or

1 tablespoon dried tarragon

2 tablespoons finely chopped scallions

2 tablespoons olive oil

Salt and pepper to taste

4 (6-oz) halibut fillets or steaks

1 lemon, cut in wedges

Combine lemon juice, zest, mustard, tarragon and scallions. Slowly stir in oil, whisking well. Add salt and pepper to taste. Arrange halibut in a shallow glass or ceramic dish and pour marinade over the fish. Turn fish to coat evenly. Cover and refrigerate for 1 hour. Preheat grill or broiler, and cook fish about 3 inches from heat source for 5 to 7 minutes on each side. Serve with lemon wedges.

TIME NEEDED: Preparation – 10 minutes, Marinating and cooking – 1 hour, 10 minutes.

✳ Cook's Notes: Halibut comes from the Middle English "haly-butte," meaning the fish to be eaten on holy days.

Per Serving: Calories 269; Total fat 10g (Sat fat 1g/ Mono fat 7g/ Poly fat 2g) Cholesterol 54mg, Sodium 414mg, Carbs 4g, Fiber 1g, Protein 36g.

Shrimp Jambalaya

A wonderful one pot meal from New Orleans

Makes 6 servings

3 cups lowfat or nonfat broth or bouillon
2 bay leaves
1 chopped onion
1 chopped green pepper
3 chopped stalks celery
2 minced cloves garlic
28 ounces canned chopped plum tomatoes
1 cup brown rice
1 tablespoon hot sauce
½ teaspoon thyme
1 pound peeled shrimp
(or 1 pound chicken breast cut into one-inch pieces)
6 chopped scallions
Salt and pepper to taste

Bring bouillon and bay leaves to a boil in large stockpot. Combine all remaining ingredients in the pot, except shrimp and scallions. Cover and reduce heat to simmer for 45 minutes, until rice is tender. Add shrimp and cook 1 to 2 minutes until pink and firm. Remove from heat and season with salt and pepper. Garnish with scallions before serving.

TIME NEEDED: 1 hour from start to finish

Cook's Notes: Why do shrimp, crab, and lobster change color when they're cooked? A pink/red pigment called astaxanthin present in the shells is altered by cooking. As it becomes freed up, the color of the shells change.

Per Serving: Calories 229; Total fat 1g (Sat fat 0g/ Mono fat 0g/ Poly fat 1g) Cholesterol 117mg, Sodium 699mg, Carbs 36g, Fiber 3g, Protein 22g.

poultry
main dishes

Most everybody loves chicken, and chicken loves you – with the skin removed, it's an excellent source of lean protein. We recommend that you keep bags of individually frozen skinless, boneless chicken breasts in your freezer to pull out as needed on short notice. Chicken breasts are extremely versatile. They are called for in many of our recipes, and they make a meal in themselves when served with a side of vegetables and salad. Sautéed, broiled, grilled, or baked, you can have dinner on the table in 15 minutes. If you prefer dark meat, no problem. Skin removed, dark meat contains only slightly more saturated fat than light meat, and it remains juicier and more flavorful through the cooking process. In Asian nations it is the darker meat that is higher priced and more sought after.

Mexican Pot Pie

On a chilly evening when you want to escape south of the border...

Makes 5 generous servings

1 teaspoon olive oil

½ pound ground chicken or turkey breast

¼ teaspoon salt or salt substitute

1 medium chopped onion

1 medium chopped green pepper

1 teaspoon chili powder

½ teaspoon ground cumin

1 15-ounce can low-sodium tomatoes, drained and chopped

1 cup canned kidney beans, rinsed and drained

1 cup thawed frozen corn

Crust:

2 ½ cups cold water

1 ½ cups cornmeal

½ teaspoon chili powder

¼ teaspoon salt or salt substitute

½ cup grated cheddar or Monterey jack cheese

Olive oil spray (optional)

Heat oil in a large non-stick skillet over medium heat. Add chicken or turkey and salt, and cook until just done. Remove from skillet.

Put onions and green pepper in skillet and cook until tender, about 10 minutes. Add chili powder, cumin, tomatoes, and beans, and cook another 5 minutes until liquid mostly evaporates. Add corn and cooked chicken or turkey, cook for 1 minute, then remove from heat. Set aside. Preheat oven to 350° F, spray a large pie pan with olive oil, and make the crust.

In a medium saucepan over medium heat, bring water, cornmeal, chili powder and salt to a boil, stirring often with a whisk. As cornmeal begins to thicken, whisk constantly until it starts to tear away from the sides of the pan – this will take about five minutes. Cool cornmeal mixture until you can handle it.

Press ²/₃ of cooled crust mixture over bottom and sides of pie pan. Spoon chicken-vegetable mixture into pan and top with cheese. Between 2 sheets of plastic wrap or waxed paper (spraying sheets with oil spray is optional), roll or press remaining cornmeal into a flat, 10-inch circle. Remove one piece of wrap or paper, flip, place on top of pie, and remove remaining wrap or paper. Spraying top of crust with olive oil spray is optional. Bake for 45 minutes or until crust is golden.

TIME NEEDED: 1½ hours, start to finish

✳ Cook's Notes: If you're in a hurry, you could make this without the crust. Serve it straight from the skillet with tortillas on the side.

Per Serving: Calories 346; Total fat 7g (Sat fat 3g/ Mono fat 3g/ Poly fat 1g) Cholesterol 33mg, Sodium 497mg, Carbs 53g, Fiber 9g, Protein 20g.

Spinach-Stuffed Chicken

The cheese and vegetable stuffing brings new life to white meat and keeps it moist.

Makes 4 servings

4 small boneless, skinless chicken breasts or
2 large (halved), (about 1 pound total)
1 teaspoon olive oil
1 medium finely chopped onion
¼ teaspoon salt
¼ teaspoon ground black pepper
1 bunch spinach, washed well, stemmed and
chopped (or 1 pound frozen chopped spinach,
thawed and drained)
½ cup fat-free ricotta cheese
¼ cup grated Parmesan cheese

In medium non-stick skillet, heat olive oil over medium heat. Add onion, salt, and pepper and sauté for 5 minutes or until tender. Add spinach to the pan and cook until wilted and all the moisture evaporates, about 5 minutes. Place in a bowl, and when cooled, add cheeses and stir well.

Preheat oven to 375° F. and spray a medium baking dish with olive oil. Carefully slice chicken breasts length-wise to create a pocket in the middle of each. (Make sure you leave the top, bottom and one side intact.) Divide spinach mixture among the chicken breasts and stuff evenly into each pocket. Spray surface of breasts with olive oil. Bake for 45 minutes, or until chicken is cooked through.

TIME NEEDED: 1 hour, 15 minutes-start to finish.

✳ Cook's Notes: For an elegant twist on roasted chicken, carefully stuff this spinach-cheese mixture under the skin of the chicken prior to roasting. Delicious!

Per Serving: Calories 235; Total fat 7g (Sat fat 3g/ Mono fat 3g/ Poly fat 1g) Cholesterol 83mg, Sodium 382mg, Carbs 7g, Fiber 2g, Protein 33g.

Oven-Fried Sesame Chicken

Needing only five to ten minutes preparation, this is a great main course for hectic days.

Makes 4 servings

2 tablespoons low-sodium soy sauce

4 small or 2 large halved boneless, skinless chicken breasts (1 pound total)

3 tablespoons sesame seeds

2 tablespoons flour

¼ teaspoon salt

¼ teaspoon pepper

Olive oil spray

Preheat oven to 400° F. Place soy sauce in shallow dish, and coat chicken. In another flat bowl, combine sesame seeds, flour, salt, and pepper. Remove chicken from the soy sauce and dredge it in the mixture. Spray 13 x 9-inch baking dish with olive oil, add chicken and spray each breast once with olive oil. Bake at 400° F. for 45 minutes or until done.

TIME NEEDED: 55 minutes start to finish.

✳ Cook's Notes: Low-sodium soy sauce has about 40 percent less sodium than regular soy sauce. It also has less flavor. An option is to use a very high-quality, aged Japanese soy sauce and dilute it with low-sodium stock or water.

Per Serving: Calories 202; Total fat 6g (Sat fat 1g/ Mono fat 3g/ Poly fat 2g) Cholesterol 69mg, Sodium 494mg, Carbs 5g, Fiber 1g, Protein 27g.

Grilled Yucatan Chicken With Citrus Yogurt

Marinate this chicken overnight and let the refrigerator work its flavor magic. The next day you can grill or broil in minutes.

Makes 4 generous servings

3½ pound fryer, cut into pieces with skin removed

2 cups plain nonfat yogurt

½ large chopped onion

3 minced cloves garlic

¼ cup fresh orange juice

2 tablespoons fresh lime juice

2 to 3 tablespoons chopped fresh cilantro

½ teaspoon ground cumin

¼ teaspoon black pepper

⅛ teaspoon cayenne

½ teaspoon salt

Place chicken in large bowl. Combine all other ingredients for marinade in small bowl. Reserve and chill one cup of the marinade. Coat chicken pieces with remaining marinade, cover and refrigerate overnight, turning occasionally. The next day, let reserved marinade warm to room temperature (or heat in the microwave for 1-2 minutes) before beginning to cook the chicken. Prepare broiler or grill for medium heat (about three inches from heat source), and cook chicken about 10 minutes on each side. (Discard any extra marinade that was on the chicken.) Place on serving dish, and top with reserved marinade.

TIME NEEDED: 15 minutes for preparation, 25 for cooking.

Per Serving: Calories 408; Total fat 11g (Sat fat 2g/ Mono fat 8g/ Poly fat 1g) Cholesterol 187mg, Sodium 558mg, Carbs 13g, Fiber 0g, Protein 72g.

Tandoori Chicken

A tandoor is a traditional Indian clay oven which achieves very high temperatures, around 550 degrees. Luckily, you don't need to travel to New Dehli to buy the special oven to get great results, but marinating is an essential step. It's best done overnight.

Makes 4 servings

1 teaspoon extra-virgin olive oil

1 to 2 teaspoons jalapeño peppers, seeds removed and finely chopped

1 chopped small onion

4 cloves garlic, peeled

2 teaspoons fresh grated ginger root, or

1 teaspoon powdered ginger

2 tablespoons coriander seeds

1 teaspoon garam masala (see Cook's Notes)

1 teaspoon turmeric

1 tablespoon lemon juice

¼ cup plain nonfat yogurt

1 pound skinless boneless chicken breasts (or 2 pounds chicken pieces, skin removed)

Combine the oil, jalapeño, onion, garlic, and spices in a blender or food processor and process on high until it achieves the consistency of a paste. Add the lemon juice and yogurt and process until smooth. Prick holes in the chicken using a fork and place in a large shallow dish. Pour the marinade over the chicken. Turn the pieces to cover all sides. Cover with plastic wrap and refrigerate for at least 2 hours, or overnight, turning occasionally. Preheat oven to 425° F. Spray a baking sheet with olive oil spray. Place chicken on the baking sheet and cook for about 30 minutes, until chicken is done and juices run clear. (May also be cooked on a grill. Cook 10 minutes on one side, turn, cook 10 minutes on the other side, then continue cooking at lower heat for another 10 minutes, if needed, until done (boneless breasts will cook faster than bone-in chicken).

TIME NEEDED: Excluding marinating, 50 minutes.

✳ Cook's Notes: Garam is the Indian word for "warm." There are many variations of garam masala, but most blends contain black pepper, cinnamon, cloves, coriander, cumin, cardamom, dried chilies, fennel, mace, nutmeg and other spices. You'll find it in ethnic markets and in the gourmet section of grocery stores.

Per Serving: Calories 176; Total fat 4g (Sat fat 1g/Mono fat 2g/Poly fat 1g) Cholesterol 69mg, Sodium 73mg, Carbs 6g, Fiber 1g, Protein 27g.

vegetarian
main dishes

You don't have to be a vegetarian to enjoy vegetarian food. In addition to being hearty and filling main dishes, smaller portions of many of these recipes can be served as a side dish, along with poultry or fish.

Pasta Shells Florentine

Four shells make a serving, but sometimes it is a good idea to boil a few extra to allow for breakage.

Makes 4 servings

16 jumbo pasta shells

10 ounces chopped spinach, fresh or frozen,
(lightly sauté until wilted or defrosted,
moisture squeezed out)

15 ounces nonfat ricotta cheese

1 tablespoon chopped basil (or 1 teaspoon dried)

Olive oil spray

3 cups marinara sauce (see recipe below)
or 1 (30-ounce) jar low-fat spaghetti sauce

¼ cup Parmesan cheese

Preheat oven to 350° F. Cook pasta shells in boiling water as directed, until al dente. Mix spinach, ricotta cheese and basil. Stuff into drained pasta shells. Spray a medium, shallow baking pan with olive oil, and spread a very thin layer of marinara sauce to coat bottom of pan. Place stuffed shells in pan, open side up, and cover with remaining sauce. Sprinkle with Parmesan, cover and bake for 45 minutes. Serving options: Top with freshly ground black pepper and a sprinkling of extra-virgin olive oil.

TIME NEEDED: 1½ hours-start to finish: 45 minutes to prepare shells and marinara sauce; 45 minutes for baking.

✳ Cook's Notes: If you don't have any ricotta cheese on hand, you can use cottage cheese. Drain it, cream it in a food processor or blender, then use as you would ricotta.

Per Serving: Calories 276; Total fat 2g (Sat fat 1g/ Mono fat trace/ Poly fat trace) Cholesterol 21mg, Sodium 636mg, Carbs 41g, Fiber 6g, Protein 25g.

Marinara Sauce

Besides Pasta Shells Florentine, use with any kind of pasta. If you aren't too concerned about sodium, adding 2 tablespoons of low-sodium soy sauce adds depth of flavor.

Makes about 5 cups

1 medium chopped onion

1 chopped green pepper

¼ pound chopped mushrooms

2 (15-ounce) cans tomatoes, chopped

3 tablespoons tomato paste

¼ cup chopped parsley (or 2 tablespoons dried)

¼ cup chopped basil (or 1 tablespoon dried)

Mix all ingredients together in a medium saucepan and simmer for at least 30 minutes.

TIME NEEDED: 45 minutes.

✳ Cook's Notes: When using as a sauce for Pasta Shells Florentine, it is best to cook the marina down until it's thick.

Per Cup: Calories 71; Total fat 0g (Sat fat 0g/ Mono fat 0g/ Poly fat 0g) Cholesterol 0mg, Sodium 334mg, Carbs 16g, Fiber 5g, Protein 3g.

Tofu "Steaks" With Grilled Onions

Tofu has one of the most unique textures in the food world and adapts itself to almost any flavor you choose to pair it with.

Makes 4 servings

1 pound extra-firm tofu

4 teaspoons low-sodium soy sauce

Olive oil cooking spray

2 sliced onions

1 teaspoon olive oil

Slice tofu lengthwise into four slices. Sprinkle each slice with 1 teaspoon soy sauce. Heat a large nonstick skillet over medium heat. Spray with olive oil and add tofu steaks. Cook for 5 minutes on each side, or until lightly browned. Remove from skillet and keep warm. Add olive oil and onions to skillet and cook, stirring often, until golden brown. If you don't like your onions crisp-tender, covering the pan briefly will make the onions softer. Divide evenly and spoon over tofu steaks.

TIME NEEDED: 20 minutes.

Per Serving: Calories 130; Total fat 7g (Sat fat 1g/ Mono fat 3g/ Poly fat 3g) Cholesterol 0mg, Sodium 210mg, Carbs 7g, Fiber 2g, Protein 10g.

168

ASK THE DOCTOR

"I've heard conflicting information about soy. Some say it's a health blessing; others say it's a bust. What do you think?"

The more I learn about soy, the more I'm sold on it. Soy is a low-fat source of high-quality protein. It protects against heart disease by lowering cholesterol (by an average of 23.2 mg/dl) and guarding against free radical damage. And soy's genistein and other isoflavones have mild estrogen-like activity that not only ease menopausal symptoms but also protect against cancer.

As for the "dark side" of soy, no, it doesn't cause cancer, although it may stimulate the growth of existing breast tumors. (The evidence on this is scant, but it's better to err on the side of caution, so women with breast cancer should avoid soy.) No, moderate intake does not harm the thyroid. (However, taking thyroid medication at the same time you're eating soy may decrease the drug's absorption, so avoid taking the two together.) Finally, no, soy formula isn't harmful to infants. (Breast milk is by far the best for babies. If it isn't available and cow's or goat's milk are not tolerated, soy formula is acceptable.)

Ratatouille Provençal

When shopping for the ingredients of this great Mediterranean classic, try to choose a small, young eggplant with undeveloped seeds, so bitterness will not be a worry.

Makes 4 servings

1 teaspoon olive oil

1 onion, cut in chunks

1 green pepper, cut in chunks

2 zucchini, cut in chunks

1 eggplant, peeled and cut in chunks

1 cup quartered mushrooms

16 ounces canned tomatoes, drained and chopped

½ teaspoon salt, seasoned salt, or salt substitute

Heat olive oil in a large nonstick skillet. Add onion and sauté for three minutes. Then add green pepper and sauté for another three minutes, repeating this pattern by adding ingredients in the following order: zucchini, eggplant, and mushrooms. Add tomatoes and salt. Boil gently and stir occasionally until some of the liquid is reduced.

TIME NEEDED: 30 minutes.

Per Serving: Calories 98; Total fat 1g (Sat fat 0g/ Mono fat 1g/ Poly fat 0g) Cholesterol 0mg, Sodium 443mg, Carbs 20g, Fiber 6g, Protein 4g.

Roasted Curried Vegetables

Find out how braising and caramelized browning can add tons of flavor that you can't get with conventional steaming.

Makes 4 servings

2 to 3 new potatoes, cut into wedges

3 medium peeled carrots, cut into ½ inch chunks

Olive oil spray

2 tablespoons olive oil (divided use)

2 medium onions, cut in wedges

¼ pound trimmed green beans, snapped in half

6 cloves peeled garlic, halved

1 red bell pepper, seeded and cut in 1-inch chunks

14 ounces canned low-sodium plum tomatoes, crushed and drained

2 tablespoons curry powder

1 cup nonfat or low fat vegetable broth

¼ teaspoon salt

Black pepper, to taste

2 tablespoons fresh lime juice

Cooked brown rice (optional)

Place rack in center of oven and preheat to 500° F. Spray a large metal roasting pan with olive oil, and add a single layer of potato wedges and carrots. Drizzle with oil, and roast for 15 minutes. Remove from oven and push potatoes and carrots to edges of pan. Add onions, green beans, garlic and red pepper to center of pan and drizzle with oil. Roast another 15 minutes. Mix tomatoes with curry powder and toss with vegetables still in roasting pan. Cook 15 minutes longer. Remove from oven and place vegetables in a large serving bowl. Put the roasting pan on stove top over rather high heat and add broth. Scrape the pan well and bring to a boil until reduced by half. Add salt, pepper and lime juice, and pour over vegetables. Serve over brown rice for a main course. Also great as a side dish.

TIME NEEDED: 1 hour.

Per Serving (excluding rice): Calories 230; Total fat 8g (Sat fat 1g/ Mono fat 6g/Poly fat 1g); Cholesterol 1mg, Sodium 580mg, Carbs 34g, Fiber 7g, Protein 6g.

side dishes

Select side dishes that complement your main course in terms of color, texture, and taste. The easiest side dishes are vegetables, steamed or cooked in the microwave for a few minutes until tender, yet crispy. (Eat the nutrient-dense vegetables discussed on page 114 often.) Starchy side dishes made with barley, long grain brown rice, quinoa, and other whole grains are fine, but don't go overboard on starches. A one-half cup to two-thirds cup serving is plenty.

Forgiven French 'Fries'

You've got to try this to believe it. Check out the 'Compare and Save' info below and see how blessedly these fries differ from the fast-food restaurant variety.

Makes 2 servings

2 medium baking potatoes

Olive oil spray

1 large egg white

2 teaspoons spice (your choice: chili, Cajun, lemon pepper, rosemary, thyme, etc.)

2 tablespoons ketchup

Preheat oven to 450° F. Slice potatoes into wedges or French fries. Spray baking sheet with olive oil. Combine egg whites with spice and use to coat potato pieces. Place sliced potatoes on baking sheet and spread them into a single layer with space in between each. Put in oven and reduce heat to 400° F. Bake for 35 - 45 minutes, turning potatoes occasionally so they brown evenly. Serve immediately with ketchup.

TIME NEEDED: 10 minutes preparation, 40 minutes baking.

Variation: To make Cheesy Forgiven French Fries, coat potatoes with egg white only. After 30 minutes in the oven, remove the baking sheet and sprinkle potatoes with 2 tablespoons freshly grated Parmesan cheese.

Per Serving: Calories 140; Total fat 1g (Sat fat 0g/ Mono fat 1g/ Poly fat 0g) Cholesterol 0mg, Sodium 213mg, Carbs 26g, Fiber 2g, Protein 4g.

173

COMPARE & SAVE

The Restaurant Version - An average order of fries at any restaurant will swamp your circulatory system with anywhere from 17 to 22 grams of fat. Hydrogenated vegetable oils are often used, resulting in hefty doses of harmful trans fatty acids, which increase risk of heart disease and a host of other maladies. The potatoes are mostly processed, precooked, and reformed, then padded with extra starches devoid of nutrition.

The Wellness Version - Would you believe only 1 gram of fat and twice the amount of protein? And real potatoes in a generous portion to boot!

Sour-Creamed Spinach

Did Popeye always take his spinach straight? There is speculation that Olive Oil enticed him with this lively variation.

Makes 2 servings

1 medium chopped onion
1 clove minced garlic
Olive oil pan spray
1 large bunch fresh chopped spinach or 10-ounce package frozen chopped spinach, thawed and drained
⅓ cup nonfat or low-fat sour cream
¼ teaspoon salt, or less if desired

Sauté onions and garlic in a medium nonstick skillet coated with olive oil. Add spinach and, if fresh, cook until wilted. (If frozen, cook until moisture evaporates.) Add sour cream to spinach mixture and salt to taste. Stir and heat to serving temperature.

TIME NEEDED: 15 minutes.

✳ Cook's Notes: It's worth paying a little extra for pre-washed and stemmed spinach. It will save you lots of time and grit. You'll be inclined to enjoy its super nutritional benefits and flavor more often.

Per Serving: Calories 100; Total fat 2g (Sat fat 0g/ Mono fat 2g/ Poly fat 0g) Cholesterol 4mg, Sodium 363mg, Carbs 14g, Fiber 5g, Protein 8g.

Curried Onion And Pepper Quinoa

Treat yourself to quinoa, a tasty, nutritious grain that is a snap to prepare.

Makes 6 servings

1 medium finely chopped onion
1 medium finely chopped red bell pepper
Olive oil pan spray
1 cup quinoa
2 cups low-sodium vegetable or chicken stock
1 teaspoon curry powder

Sauté onion and red pepper in nonstick saucepan sprayed with olive oil over medium heat for 3-5 minutes. Rinse quinoa and add to pan with 2 cups stock and curry powder. Bring to a boil, reduce heat and simmer for about 15 minutes, until water is absorbed and grains have turned from white to transparent.

TIME NEEDED: 30 minutes

✳ Cook's Notes: Quinoa (pronounced "keen-wah") is an ancient grain native to the Andes mountains of Peru. It is considered the highest source of protein among grains and is very well tolerated (even by people who have digestive difficulties).

Per Serving: Calories 131; Total fat 2g (Sat fat 0g/ Mono fat 1g/ Poly fat 1g) Cholesterol 0mg, Sodium 214mg, Carbs 23g, Fiber 2g, Protein 5g.

Harvest Barley Pilaf

Vegetable-grain mixes are a dynamite combo, bringing new life to both.

Makes 4 servings

8 ounces sliced mushrooms

1 medium chopped zucchini

1 medium chopped onion

Olive oil pan spray

1 cup pearl barley

2 cups low-sodium vegetable or chicken stock

Preheat oven to 350° F. In a medium skillet sprayed with olive oil, sauté mushrooms, zucchini, and onion for 5 minutes over medium heat. Next, add barley and 2 cups stock to the pan, raise heat, and bring to a quick boil. Spray a 2-quart baking dish with olive oil. Add all ingredients, stir well, cover, and cook in oven for about 30 minutes. Check occasionally and add a little water if needed.

TIME NEEDED: 45 minutes.

✳ Cook's Notes: Pilafs can either be baked, as this recipe suggests, or cooked on the stove in a covered saucepan. If you chose the stovetop method, make sure to cook it over very low heat to avoid burning.

Per Serving: Calories 224; Total fat 2g (Sat fat 0g/ Mono fat 1g/ Poly fat 1g) Cholesterol 0mg, Sodium 319mg, Carbs 46g, Fiber 10g, Protein 8g.

Soy-Sesame Broccoli

You can never have too many quick recipes for super-nutritious broccoli.

Makes 3 servings

1 large bunch broccoli

2 teaspoons sesame oil

1 tablespoon low-sodium soy sauce

2 teaspoons fresh lemon juice

1 tablespoon toasted sesame seeds

Separate broccoli into florets, and peel and slice stems into 1/4-inch pieces. Steam until al dente, about 8 minutes, and drain. Mix sesame oil, soy sauce and lemon, pour over broccoli, and toss well. Top with sesame seeds and serve.

TIME NEEDED: 10 minutes.

Per Serving: Calories 105; Total fat 5g (Sat fat 1g/ Mono fat 2g/ Poly fat 2g) Cholesterol 0mg, Sodium 255mg, Carbs 12g, Fiber 6g, Protein 7g.

German Red Cabbage With Apples

Sweet cabbage, sweet onions, and sweet-tart apples make sweet harmony.

Makes 3 servings

1 medium sliced onion

1 medium peeled, cored, sliced apple

1 tablespoon olive oil

4 cups shredded red cabbage

¼ teaspoon salt

¼ cup dry red wine

3 tablespoons red wine vinegar

2 tablespoons low-fat or
nonfat sour cream (optional)

In a large saucepan, sauté onion and apple in oil for 5 minutes. Add remaining ingredients, stir, reduce heat, cover, and simmer. Cook about 20 minutes, stirring occasionally, until tender but not mushy. Drain excess liquid and serve. Top with sour cream if desired.

TIME NEEDED: 25 minutes

✳ Cook's Notes: Americans like to use fruit in pies and other desserts or in fruit salads – and that's about all. We hope this recipe will convince you of the versatility of apples.

Per Serving: Calories 132; Total fat 5g (Sat fat 1g/ Mono fat 3g/ Poly fat 1g) Cholesterol 2mg, Sodium 220mg, Carbs 18g, Fiber 4g, Protein 2g.

desserts

Everybody needs an indulgence now and then, and these desserts fit the bill. We think you'll like these recipes – they're tasty but not overly sweet, and because so many of them are fruit based, they're full of nutrition as well.

Cranberry-Apple Crisp

Of all our desserts, this one receives the most raves.

Makes 8 servings

Olive oil spray

3 peeled and cored apples, thinly sliced

1 cup fresh or frozen cranberries

⅓ cup frozen apple juice concentrate

⅓ cup whole wheat flour

1 cup old-fashioned oatmeal, uncooked

2 tablespoons hazelnut oil

1 teaspoon cinnamon

¼ cup chopped walnuts

2 tablespoons honey or brown rice syrup

Preheat oven to 350° F. Spray an 8 x 8-inch baking dish with olive oil spray. Mix apples and cranberries in a medium mixing bowl. Pour apple juice concentrate over fruit. Stir well and pour into baking dish. In another mixing bowl, mix flour, oatmeal, oil, cinnamon, walnuts, and honey. Sprinkle over fruit in baking dish. Bake at 350° F for 40-50 minutes, or until oatmeal is brown and apples are bubbly.

TIME NEEDED: 1 hour.

Per Serving: Calories 172; Total fat 6g (Sat fat 1g/ Mono fat 1g/ Poly fat 4g) Cholesterol 0mg, Sodium 4mg, Carbs 25g, Fiber 4g, Protein 3g.

Ambrosia Delight

The citrus flavor of the Grand Marnier magnifies the natural flavor of each and every fruit.

Makes 6 servings

1 cup sliced bananas

1 cup fresh pineapple chunks

1 cup berries (blueberries, strawberries, etc., or a mixture of your choice)

1 cup seedless green grapes

1 cup chopped pear

1 orange, juiced

2 tablespoons Grand Marnier or your favorite liquor (optional)

Stevia or xylitol to taste

Combine fruits in a serving bowl. Mix orange juice, Grand Marnier, and sweetener in a small bowl. Pour over fruit, stir and serve.

TIME NEEDED: 10 minutes

✳ Cook's Notes: This simple dessert becomes simply elegant when served in wine or parfait glasses.

Per Serving: Calories 121; Total fat 0g (Sat fat 0g/ Mono fat 0g/ Poly fat 0g) Cholesterol 0mg, Sodium 5mg, Carbs 28g, Fiber 3g, Protein 1g.

Cranberry-Walnut Baked Apples

For an added treat, you might try topping these traditional baked treats with Vanilla Cream (see recipe on page 48).

Makes 4 servings

4 medium baking apples (Granny Smith or another tart apple; do not use Delicious)
4 teaspoons frozen apple juice concentrate
¼ teaspoon cinnamon
⅛ teaspoon nutmeg
8 teaspoons dried cranberries
4 teaspoons chopped walnuts

Preheat oven to 350° F. Core apples from stem side almost through the bottom. Remove ½ inch of apple peel from top of each apple. Mix apple juice concentrate with cinnamon and nutmeg. Fill each apple cavity with 1 teaspoon apple concentrate, 2 teaspoons cranberries, and 1 teaspoon walnuts. Place in a small baking dish. Pour ½ inch water around apples. Bake for 20 minutes, or until apples are soft but still holding their shape. Serve warm or cold.

TIME NEEDED: 30 minutes.

✱ Cook's Notes: Use your favorite apples for this recipe, as long as they aren't Delicious or Golden Delicious —these apples get too soft and mushy during baking.

Per Serving: Calories 107; Total fat 1g (Sat fat 0g/ Mono fat 0g/ Poly fat 1g) Cholesterol 0mg, Sodium 1mg, Carbs 24g, Fiber 4g, Protein 1g.

Granny Smith Cake

This rustic country cake leaves you wanting for nothing, except a good cup of tea to go with it.

Makes 8 servings

4 Granny Smith apples (about 2 pounds)
Olive oil spray
½ cup whole wheat flour (preferred), or unbleached all-purpose
⅓ cup xylitol
1 tablespoon baking powder
⅛ teaspoon salt
½ teaspoon vanilla extract
2 large eggs, lightly beaten
2 tablespoons hazelnut oil
⅓ cup low-fat 2% milk
5 pecan halves (optional garnish)
1 tablespoon powdered sugar

Peel and core apples and cut into thin wedges. Preheat oven to 400°F. Spray a 9-inch springform pan or cake pan with olive oil spray. Combine flour, xylitol, baking powder and salt in a large bowl. Stir well. Add vanilla, eggs, oil, and milk, stirring just until blended. Reserve about 10 slices of apple and add the rest to batter, stirring only until coated.

Pour batter into prepared pan and arrange reserved apple slices in radiating flower pattern on top.

If desired, arrange pecans in center. Bake 20-25 minutes, until golden brown and firm to the touch. Cool on rack for 10 minutes before removing from springform. When cool, sift powdered sugar over top.

Time needed: 45 minutes.

Per Serving: Calories 126; Total fat 5g (Sat fat 1g/ Mono fat 2g/ Poly fat 2g) Cholesterol 48mg, Sodium 53mg, Carbs 23g, Fiber 3g, Protein 3g.

Summer Evening Cobbler

Picture yourself out on the porch swing with a bowl of this cobbler, two spoons, and your sweetheart. If you don't have a swing or a sweetie, you can still enjoy this delightful dessert.

Makes 6 servings

Olive oil pan spray

3 tablespoons tapioca granules

1½ cups grape juice (purple or white)

1 teaspoon vanilla

2 peeled and sliced pears

1 cup berries (your choice or mixed)

¾ cup oatmeal

¼ cup raw sesame seeds

1½ tablespoons hazelnut oil

(may substitute other oil)

2 tablespoons brown rice syrup or honey

Preheat oven to 350° F. Coat a pie pan with olive oil spray. Mix tapioca with juice and vanilla and pour into pie pan. Layer the pear slices, followed by berries, on top of the tapioca mixture. Mix oatmeal, sesame seeds, oil, and brown rice syrup until well blended. Sprinkle on top of fruit. Bake for 30 minutes. Serve warm.

TIME NEEDED: 45 minutes.

Per Serving: Calories 231; Total fat 7g (Sat fat 1g/ Mono fat 4g/ Poly fat 2g) Cholesterol 0mg, Sodium 13mg, Carbs 39g, Fiber 4g, Protein 3g.

THE DOCTOR IS IN:

Tapioca comes from the roots of the cassava plant, which is native to South America. Compounds in cassava are being investigated as a treatment for cancer.

183

Poached Ginger Pears

Sweet and simple, yet robust and satisfying. The brown rice syrup gives a wonderful body and flavor to the sauce.

Makes 4 small or 2 large servings

2 cups water

¼ cup brown rice syrup

¼ cup xylitol

8 thin slices of fresh ginger, about 1-inch in diameter

4 peeled, halved and cored pears, ripe yet firm

Combine water, brown rice syrup, xylitol, and ginger in a large saucepan. Bring to a boil and stir until xylitol dissolves, about 2 minutes. Add pears, reduce heat, and simmer uncovered for 10 minutes, turning fruit once. Remove pears with slotted spoon and place in individual serving bowls. Boil syrup until it thickens to resemble a light syrup. Remove ginger pieces and pour over pears. Can be served hot, chilled, or at room temperature.

TIME NEEDED: 30 minutes, start to finish.

Cook's Notes: Never store unripe pears in the refrigerator – this will interfere with the ripening process. And don't let them ripen too much. The peak of ripeness is characterized by firmness with a slight give.

Based on 4 servings: Calories 140; Total fat 0g (Sat fat 0g/ Mono fat 0g/ Poly fat 0g) Cholesterol 0mg, Sodium 2mg, Carbs 35g, Fiber 5g, Protein 1g.

Glycemic Index of Common Foods

Slow-burning, nutrient-dense, low-glycemic carbohydrates are the foundation of the recipes in the *Quick & Healthy* cookbook and should comprise the bulk of your diet.

Low-to-Moderate Glycemic Foods (Enjoy often)

- All fresh and frozen fruits (Go easy on ripe bananas, which have a higher glycemic index, and limit fruit juices, which are highly concentrated.)
- Dried apricots
- All fresh and frozen green vegetables
- All beans, peas and legumes
- Whole, unprocessed grains such as barley, wheat kernels, bulgur, and quinoa
- Whole-grain cereals like oatmeal (slow-cooking), wheat and rye flakes, rice and oat bran, and 100% bran cold cereals like Bran Buds, All-Bran
- Sprouted grain, stone-ground whole wheat, whole-grain pumpernickel and rye breads
- Pasta cooked al dente, until just tender (overcooking raises the glycemic index)
- Dairy (low-fat or nonfat milk, yogurt, and cottage cheese preferred)
- Soy milk

High-Glycemic Foods (Eat sparingly)

- Dried fruits (except for dried apricots)
- Root vegetables (white potatoes, beets, parsnips, turnips, rutabaga, potatoes; new potatoes have the lowest glycemic index)
- Most breads (white, whole wheat, bagels)
- Most cereals (Cream of Wheat, instant oatmeal, most cold cereals)
- Rice (long-grain brown rice and brown basmati rice have the lowest glycemic index)
- Most snack foods (corn chips, rice cakes, pretzels)

  (From *The New Glucose Revolution* by Jennie Brand-Miller et al, 2003, Marlowe and Company, New York, NY; and http://www.netrition.com)

Appendix: Antioxidants and Other Protective Micronutrients in Food

Antioxidants

Although you may be unaware of it, you are under assault. The culprits are free radicals, and believe it or not, they attack each of your cells thousands of times a day. Just hearing their name induces visions of wild scavengers looting and pillaging. Actually, this is pretty close to the truth. Free radicals are unstable byproducts that are created as your cells burn oxygen. They kick off a chain reaction of destruction that, were it not for natural protectors called antioxidants, would do untold damage to your cells. Antioxidants step in to stabilize marauding free radicals and end their cycle of cellular damage.

Free radical-induced damage is at the root of many common degenerative diseases like heart and kidney problems, hardening of the arteries, and arthritis. It is also a driving force behind aging. Obviously, having an ample supply of antioxidants on hand to counter free radicals is crucial. Some antioxidants are produced in your body. However, the more you get from dietary and supplement sources, the better.

Antioxidants are only one of the protective nutrients you get when you eat a healthful diet. All species of plants produce compounds which, like fingerprints, are unique only to them. They protect the plant from everyday stresses such as weather, ultraviolet light, insects, fungi, bacteria, and even abnormal plant cell growth. When we eat plants, these compounds, which are called phytonutrients, have beneficial effects in our bodies as well.

Following is a list of some of the most potent antioxidants, vitamins, minerals, and phytonutrients and the foods in which they are found.

Powerhouses of Protective Micronutrients

ALLICIN
Allicin and other sulfur compounds lower blood pressure, reduce cholesterol, and inhibit the growth of microbes and cancer cells. These sulfur compounds also act as antioxidants.
Best sources: Garlic, onions, leeks, chives, and scallions

ALPHA- AND GAMMA-CAROTENE
These members of the cartenoid family actually have more antioxidant activity than their better-known cousin, beta-carotene.
Best sources: Carrots, squash, green peppers, potatoes, and corn

ANTHOCYANIDINS

Anthocyanidins strengthen the blood vessels and protect them from free radical damage. They also help improve circulation.

Best sources: Blueberries, raspberries, strawberries, cherries, and plums

BETA-CAROTENE

One of the best-known phytonutrients, this potent antioxidant protects the skin from the damaging effects of UV radiation, strengthens the immune system, and enhances vision. It is also converted in the body into vitamin A when needed.

Best sources: Carrots, sweet potatoes, squash, and other yellow-orange fruits and vegetables

BETA-GLUCAN

This water-soluble fiber has been shown in clinical studies to reduce the adverse effects of high-fat meals on the arteries and to lower LDL cholesterol.

Best sources: Oatmeal and barley

BIOFLAVONOIDS

Bioflavonoids help strengthen the capillary walls and improve their resistance to changes in pressure. They also improve the absorption of vitamin C and work synergistically with this antioxidant.

Best sources: Citrus fruits, including oranges, lemons, limes, tangerines, and grapefruit

CALCIUM

This mineral is required for the building and maintenance of strong bones. It is also involved in the regulation of heart beat and muscle contractions.

Best sources: Dairy foods, canned sardines, collard greens, and other leafy greens

ELLAGIC ACID

Ellagic acid is a strong antioxidant. It also has potent anti-cancer properties because it inhibits DNA mutations.

Best sources: Cherries, pomegranates, raspberries, strawberries, blueberries, and walnuts

FOLIC ACID (FOLATE OR FOLACIN)

This B-complex vitamin keeps homocysteine levels in check. High levels of homocysteine increase risk of heart attack, stroke, and Alzheimer's disease. Folic acid also protects against spina bifida and other neural tube birth defects.

Best sources: Beans, spinach, oatmeal, asparagus, avocados, and cruciferous vegetables

LIGNANS

Lignans are a type of fiber with potent anti-cancer activity. They bind to estrogen in the gastrointestinal tract and help eliminate it from the body, thus decreasing excessive estrogen exposure and risk of breast cancer.

Best sources: Flaxseed and other grains and seeds

LUTEIN

This carotenoid is especially abundant in eye tissue. In a recent study, individuals who had the highest intake of lutein had a 43 percent lower incidence of macular degeneration than those with the lowest intake.

Best sources: Green, leafy vegetables such as kale, collards, and spinach

LYCOPENE

Lycopene may be the most impressive cancer fighter of all the carotenoids. Studies have shown that people who consume five or more servings per week of cooked tomato products or have a high serum level of lycopene have a significantly lower risk of cancers of the prostate, lung, colon, stomach, and pancreas. It is also protective against heart disease and asthma.

Best sources: Tomatoes (tomato sauce, paste, juice and other cooked tomato products are the most concentrated sources), watermelon, and guava

INDOLES

Indoles such as indole-3-carbinol lower levels of harmful estrogens that can promote tumor growth in hormone-sensitive cells, especially the cells of the breast, making them a powerful weapon against breast cancer.

Best sources: Cruciferous vegetables like broccoli, Brussels sprouts, and cabbage

ISOFLAVONES

Isoflavones are powerful antioxidants that protect the arteries and discourage LDL oxidation. Isoflavones such as genistein also have mild estrogenic activity and are sometimes called phytoestrogens. They displace stronger, more dangerous forms of estrogen at receptor sites in the body and thus protect against cancer of the breast, endothelium, and prostate.

Best source: Soybeans

LIMINOIDS

These phytonutrients help normalize cholesterol levels and are particularly protective against tumor growth.

Best sources: Lemons, limes, and other citrus fruits

MAGNESIUM

This important mineral works with calcium to build bone tissue. It helps regulate heart rhythm, relax the arteries, and maintain normal blood pressure. It is also involved in hundreds of enzymatic reactions in the body.

Best sources: Almonds, hazelnuts, sunflower seeds, tofu, Swiss chard, and other leafy greens

OMEGA-3 FATTY ACIDS

These essential fatty acids improve circulation, inhibit the formation of blood clots, protect the arteries, help normalize blood pressure and heart rhythm, and lower cholesterol and triglycerides. They also nourish the brain and improve mood and memory.

Best sources: Fatty fish like salmon, mackerel, tuna, herring, sardines, anchovies and trout, and flaxseeds

OMEGA-6 FATTY ACIDS

Omega-6 fatty acids work in concert with omega-3's to create stable cell membranes and a balanced inflammatory response.

Best sources: Nuts, seeds, grains, and unrefined nut butters and vegetable oils

PHYTOSTEROLS

These fatty compounds help lower cholesterol levels by blocking the uptake of cholesterol in the intestines. They also protect against cancer and help fight heart disease.

Best sources: Soybeans, whole grains, and green vegetables

POLYPHENOLS

Polyphenols inhibit cancer by blocking the formation of cancer-causing compounds and detoxifying carcinogens. They also have powerful antioxidant and antibacterial properties. In addition, they improve blood flow and discourage blood clotting.

Best sources: Green and black tea, grapes, wine

POTASSIUM

This mineral helps lower blood pressure and reduces risk of stroke. High intake of potassium balances high intake of sodium, which is so common in today's diet.

Best sources: All vegetables and fruits, especially bananas, beet greens, avocados, dried apricots and beans

QUERCETIN

This bioflavonoid inhibits the release of histamine and helps prevent hay fever and other allergic reactions. It also has anti-inflammatory activity and has proven benefits for prostatitis. In addition, it is a potent radical scavenger, has antiviral activity, and is an effective anti-tumor agent against a wide range of cancers, including cancers of the breast, ovaries, colon, rectum, and brain.

Best sources: Onions, apples, red wine, and green tea

SELENIUM

In addition to being a potent antioxidant, selenium protects against heart disease and inhibits the replication of viruses and cancer cells. Adequate intake of selenium is associated with a dramatically reduced risk of cancer.

Best sources: Brazil nuts, seafood, poultry, wheat germ, and brown rice

SULFORAPHANE

This sulfur-based nutrient protects against cancer by boosting the production of cancer-blocking enzymes. In one study, sulforaphane neutralized carcinogens before they could trigger tumor growth.

Best sources: Broccoli, Brussels sprouts, cabbage, and other cruciferous vegetables

VITAMIN C

This very important antioxidant supports your blood vessels, immune system, and virtually every cell in your body. Studies have shown that eating more vitamin C-rich fruits and vegetables protects against heart disease.

Best sources: Citrus fruits, strawberries, peppers, guavas, and leafy greens

VITAMIN E

The most active fat-soluble antioxidant in the body, a high intake of vitamin E is associated with a reduced risk of heart attack.

Best sources: Nuts, seeds, whole grains, and vegetable oils

ZINC

Zinc is a trace mineral that boosts immune function and wound healing. It is also necessary for growth and development and for the maintenance of the senses of taste and smell.

Best sources: Oysters, crab, meat, and wheat germ

Index

Credits

Text and Recipes by Julian Whitaker, MD
and his staff at the Whitaker Wellness Institute

Editor: Randolph Mann

Book Design: Scoot Design, San Francisco

Photography: Lisa Keenan Photography

Stockfood, GettyOne Images, FoodPix.

Food Styling: Suzanne Carreiro

ISBN 1-930603-08-8

Printed and bound in Singapore